W9-BCB-779

ponds
fountains & waterfalls

SMART GUIDE

CREATIVE HOMEOWNER®, Upper Saddle River, New Jersey

SMART GUIDE: PONDS, FOUNTAINS & WATERFALLS

MANAGING EDITOR	Fran Donegan
SENIOR GRAPHIC DESIGNER	Glee Barre
CONTRIBUTING EDITOR	Miranda Smith
JUNIOR EDITOR	Angela Hanson
PHOTO COORDINATOR	Mary Dolan
INDEXER	Schroeder Indexing Services
DIGITAL IMAGING SPECIALIST	Frank Dyer
SMART GUIDE® SERIES COVER DESIGN	Clarke Barre
FRONT COVER PHOTOGRAPHY	Jerry Pavia Photography Inc.

CREATIVE HOMEOWNER

VICE PRESIDENT AND PUBLISHER	Timothy O. Bakke
MANAGING EDITOR	Fran J. Donegan
ART DIRECTOR	David Geer
PRODUCTION COORDINATOR	Sara M. Markowitz

Current Printing (last digit)
10 9 8 7 6 5 4 3 2

Manufactured in the United States of America

Smart Guide: Ponds, Fountains & Waterfalls, Second Edition
Library of Congress Control Number: 2009921215
ISBN-10: 1-58011-463-6
ISBN-13: 978-1-58011-463-9

CREATIVE HOMEOWNER®
A Division of Federal Marketing Corp.
24 Park Way
Upper Saddle River, NJ 07458
www.creativehomeowner.com

Metric Conversion

Length

1 inch	25.4 mm
1 foot	0.3048 m
1 yard	0.9144 m
1 mile	1.61 km

Area

1 square inch	645 mm²
1 square foot	0.0929 m²
1 square yard	0.8361 m²
1 acre	4046.86 m²
1 square mile	2.59 km²

Volume

1 cubic inch	16.3870 cm³
1 cubic foot	0.03 m³
1 cubic yard	0.77 m³

Common Lumber Equivalents
Sizes: Metric cross sections are so close to their U.S. sizes, as noted below, that for most purposes they may be considered equivalents.

Dimensional	1 x 2	19 x 38 mm
lumber	1 x 4	19 x 89 mm
	2 x 2	38 x 38 mm
	2 x 4	38 x 89 mm
	2 x 6	38 x 140 mm
	2 x 8	38 x 184 mm
	2 x 10	38 x 235 mm
	2 x 12	38 x 286 mm
Sheet	4 x 8 ft.	1200 x 2400 mm
sizes	4 x 10 ft.	1200 x 3000 mm
Sheet	¼ in.	6 mm
thicknesses	⅜ in.	9 mm
	½ in.	12 mm
	¾ in.	19 mm
Stud/joist	16 in. o.c.	400 mm o.c.
spacing	24 in. o.c.	600 mm o.c.

Capacity

1 fluid ounce	29.57 mL
1 pint	473.18 mL
1 quart	1.14 L
1 gallon	3.79 L

Weight

1 ounce	28.35g
1 pound	0.45kg

Temperature
Celsius = Fahrenheit − 32 x ⅝
Fahrenheit = Celsius x 1.8 + 32

contents

safety first

All projects and procedures in this book have been reviewed for safety; still it is not possible to overstate the importance of working carefully. What follows are reminders for plant care and project safety. Always use common sense.

- *Always* use caution, care, and good judgment when following the procedures in this book.

- *Always* determine locations of underground utility lines before you dig, and then avoid them by a safe distance. Buried lines may be for gas, electricity, communications, or water. Contact local utility companies who will help you map their lines.

- *Always* read and heed tool manufacturer instructions.

- *Always* ensure that the electrical setup is safe; be sure that no circuit is overloaded and that all power tools and electrical outlets are properly grounded and protected by a ground-fault circuit interrupter (GCFI). Do not use power tools in wet locations.

- *Always* wear eye protection when using chemicals, sawing wood, pruning trees and shrubs, using power tools, and striking metal onto metal or concrete.

- *Always* consider nontoxic and least toxic methods of addressing unwanted plants, plant pests, and plant diseases before resorting to toxic methods. Follow package application and safety instructions carefully.

- *Always* read labels on chemicals, solvents, and other products; provide ventilation; heed warnings.

- *Always* wear a hard hat when working in situations with potential for injury from falling tree limbs.

- *Always* wear appropriate gloves in situations in which your hands could be injured by rough surfaces, sharp edges, thorns, or poisonous plants.

- *Always* protect yourself against ticks, which can carry Lyme disease. Wear light-colored, long-sleeved shirts and pants. Inspect yourself for ticks after every session in the garden.

- *Always* wear a disposable face mask or a special filtering respirator when creating sawdust or working with toxic gardening substances.

- *Always* keep your hands and other body parts away from the business end of blades, cutters, and bits.

- *Always* obtain approval from local building officials before undertaking construction of permanent structures.

- *Never* employ herbicides, pesticides, or toxic chemicals unless you have determined with certainty that they were developed for the specific problem you hope to remedy.

- *Never* allow bystanders to approach work areas where they might by injured by workers or work-site hazards. Make sure all work sites are well marked.

- *Never* work with power tools when you are tired, or under the influence of alcohol or drugs.

- *Never* carry sharp or pointed tools, such as knives or saws, in your pocket.

introduction

Of all the things you could add to your landscape, water features, such as ponds, fountains, and waterfalls, are the most dramatic and rewarding. What else provides sound, movement, reflections, and the opportunity to attract animals and use plants in entirely new ways? This book has been organized to both inspire and provide you with practical, hands-on guidance. It shows how to plan and build ponds, water-

courses, waterfalls, and fountains. You'll learn how to integrate them into your landscape, how to select the right products to keep them functioning, how to build the water features you have selected, and how to add plants, wildlife, lighting, and other accessories to complete your project.

chapter 1
planning your pond

THINK ABOUT WHY YOU WANT A WATER GARDEN.
If your ideas are vague, this chapter will help. We will examine the factors you should consider in creating a water feature, pose questions you should ask yourself, and suggest possible answers. Planning will help prevent first-time mistakes and ensure that your water feature will bring you pleasure, not problems.

Consider Your Lifestyle

When professional landscape designers begin a project, they ask their clients about their lifestyle and goals. These questions might include: What do you want to do in your garden? Do you spend a lot of time outdoors enjoying your property, or is your yard more of a backdrop for your house? Do you want your pond to beautify the view from inside the house or to dress up your entryway for the pleasure of your guests?

If your outside time is limited to sitting on the patio reading the newspaper or discussing the day's events with your spouse, a small container garden or independent fountain may be just right for you.

Entertainment. If a patio or deck is the center of your outdoor life, a water garden offers great potential as both a mood setter and a conversation piece. A small water feature softly bubbling in a corner is relaxing and stimulates quiet conversation, while a big splashy one may heighten excitement and energy. Place a raised pond along one side of a deck or even in the center if it won't impede traffic, and finish the pond a wide edge so that you and your guests can sit and admire the fish and plant life unique to a water garden. If your patio looks out over a long, narrow backyard, you can make your landscape look even deeper if you install a long formal pool or place a pond at the far end to create a focal point. Keep the lines of a more remote water feature clean and bold so that the design can speak from a distance.

If you have young children, you may want to incorporate a pond they can explore and enjoy. Even shallow ponds pose a safety hazard for toddlers, however. Safer alternatives include a small fountain burbling in a shallow circle of pebbles or a waterfall that empties into a shallow stream.

Landscaping. If you enjoy puttering in your garden, a water feature can be as labor-intensive as you like. As with any other part of your landscape, a pond offers endless possibilities for adding plants or rearranging those you already have, with the added enticement of fish and other pond life. Or you may

The water lily's color and fragrance can be the inspiration for creating a lush water garden.

make your pond a backdrop for your existing landscaping. For example, one gardener used a backhoe to dig a half-acre pond to enhance a collection of unusual trees and shrubs; their beautiful colors and shapes are now reflected in the view from his sunroom window.

Siting Your Water Feature

Even on the smallest property, you may discover several spots for a water feature. In selecting the site, consider where the water feature will provide the most pleasure while still being practical. You also need to ensure that the water garden looks like a natural part of the landscape, a task that involves both careful siting and additional plantings.

Aesthetic Considerations

Your view of the pond will greatly determine how much you enjoy it. Ideally, you want to be able to watch it change throughout the seasons, from as many vantage points as possible. From indoors, you can enjoy your pond even in inclement weather: the reflection of scudding clouds, the splash of raindrops, the formation of ice.

Before you dig, make sure you'll be able to see the water feature from your intended viewing location. For example, if you want to see the pond from a breakfast nook, make sure you'll get a good view while sitting at the table. When siting the pond, you can preview its size and location by using plastic drop cloths or some old sheets. Lay the material down in various places in your garden to experiment with positioning and shape.

Hidden Water Feature. You can also employ a landscape-design trick known as evoking a sense of mystery. Instead of putting the pond in full view, hide it so that just a teasing glimpse beckons and invites strollers to investigate. Between the path and the pond, plant tall grasses or a hedge of lacy conifers—or erect a bamboo screen or vine-covered trellis—allowing just a shimmer of water to hint at what lies beyond.

A completely hidden water feature offers other advantages. It can be a welcome retreat where you can enjoy the sights and sounds of nature and forget for a while the chores that await you. To make this area even more of an outdoor "room," add a flagstone or gravel floor, a table and chairs, and lighting for nighttime enjoyment. Total enclosure of a water feature is especially appealing if you are surrounded by sights and sounds that you want to block out, such as heavy traffic and nearby neighbors.

plantings around your own house. A carefully trimmed hedge can reveal the top of a church steeple or tall trees while blocking out less attractive elements. If there is a nice view from only one side of the pond, draw attention to it with a small area of stone, brick, or wood decking. A bench, lantern, or other decorative object will suggest a place of welcome, even if it isn't functional; the bench can be a rustic child-size seat, and the lantern can be stone or a battered antique.

Reflections. When considering views from your pond, remember that you will want to look not only across it but also into it. What will be reflected in the pond, and how will those reflections change throughout the day and throughout the seasons? Can you capture sunrises or sunsets? The full moon in June? What about azaleas in spring or maple leaves in autumn? Some experts suggest placing a large mirror on the prospective pond site to give you some idea of how water might reflect light and color. If you're a photographer, you know it's easier to see the image well if you keep the sun behind you, and this is also true of ponds. If your view is straight into the sun, all you'll see in your pond is reflected glare.

Consider seasonal changes. Even less-than-ideal weather can paint beautiful portraits in and around your pond.

Concealing your pond on one or more sides can evoke an exciting sense of mystery.

Existing Features. Another important consideration when choosing a site is how easily the water feature can be integrated into the existing landscape. Determine which of your current yard features will complement the pond and which will detract from it. Before deciding on a site, examine the views from all angles. For example, siting the pond in one area of the yard may mean that you would need to remove one or more large trees or shrubs to allow you to see the pond from the house. Or you may find eyesores such as an old shed that will need to be razed or a bare house wall that should be disguised with vines. If you have decided on a particular size for your pond, you'll need to take that into consideration when choosing the site. For example, a small pond can get lost next to an immense deck. A large pond stuffed into a small side yard may also look out of proportion.

Borrow Views. Before you wall yourself off completely, however, see whether there are any views worth "borrowing" for your design. Borrowing a pleasing but more distant view is like adding a window to your garden room. It makes a small enclosure seem larger without sacrificing privacy. Decide which elements of the wider world to allow into your cozy spot. Consider the potential view from each side of the pond to see what pleasant vista you could incorporate—the corner of a neighbor's lot with a perennial bed or expanse of green lawn, or a view toward

Many ponds look like a hole in the ground with a necklace of stones, and gardeners don't solve the problem by adding a starched collar of plants. Ponds look more natural anchored to an existing feature such as a large boulder or a small specimen tree, or tucked into the curve of a perennial or shrub border.

If you don't have such a feature, you may need to create one. Consider connecting the pond to the rest of the garden by echoing other elements in the landscape. Incorporate bricks in the pond's design to complement a brick house, or a deck surround that mimics the deck on the house. The pond's shape can mirror a planting bed, or be surrounded by the same types of shrubs as planted elsewhere.

Paths. Paths are another way to tie your pond to the rest of your landscape and to your home. You can choose informal gravel paths or the more structured look of brick or stone walkways.

Practical Considerations

Beauty isn't all you need to think about in choosing a place for your pond. Climate, existing structures and trees, and the general lay of the land can all determine whether your pond is heaven or a headache.

Sun and Shade. If you want flowering plants to be an important part of your water garden, you need to place the pond where it will get at least six hours of sunlight a day. Water lilies in particular don't bloom well with less sun (although there are a few varieties that will perform in partial shade).

There is a downside to too much sun, however. Water will evaporate quickly from a pond in full sun in hot climates. Sun encourages algae and, if the pond is small, can heat the water too much for fish. (See "Controlling Algae" on page 70 for some helpful tips.) For this reason, small water features—and especially tub gardens—need shadier sites. For larger ponds, provide shade with floating plants or situate small trees to lend dappled shade across at least part of the pond surface. Use rocks to create overhangs where fish can keep cool and protect themselves from predators. Remember that nature creates inviting pools even in the heart of heavily shaded woodlands. You can, too, by choosing appropriate plants.

If you've only recently moved to your property, keep track of the sun's position throughout each season of the year, including the amount of sun and shade in different parts of the yard. Use this information to judge which site will best meet the needs for your water feature.

Views. A bench or other seating sends a visual message that "this is a lovely place to be." Place it to capture the best view across your pond.

Complying with Local Regulations

Make sure your plans comply with local building codes. Depending on where you live, regulations may deem a pond beyond a certain depth a safety hazard and, just as with swimming pools, require that it be fenced in. Fencing may be necessary for ponds as shallow as 2 feet. Most zoning boards consider a pond a structure, and as such there may also be rules pertaining to its placement and size.

If you intend to redesign a natural water feature such as a pond or stream, you would be altering a wetland, and that means you must apply for a permit, usually with your local conservation commission, department of natural resources, or other environmental review agency. This usually involves preparing a complex and legally demanding environmental impact statement.

Wind. Ponds should have some degree of protection from wind, which like sun will hasten the rate of evaporation. Wind can also blow leaves and other debris into your pond, spoil the graceful flow of a fountain, and knock over tall plants in containers. If possible, choose a sheltered site that is protected from wind by a hill, trees, a building, or a fence. If your yard is windy and has no sheltered spot, you'll need to create some type of a windbreak. Surprisingly, a barrier that lets some wind through is more effective than a solid wall or closed-board fence, which allows wind to blow across its top and resume full force a few feet beyond the structure. Depending on the style of your pond, you can create an effective windbreak by installing an open-board or lattice fence, a screen of native evergreens, or an attractive flowering hedge.

If you decide to use trees to create shade or a windbreak, select and site them carefully so that they don't end up providing more shade than you desire, or cause other problems, such as dropping leaves into the water or damaging the pond's liner with their roots. Before you plant, learn about the growth rate and mature size of any species you're considering. For example, Leyland cypress (*xCupressocyparis leylandii*) is often recommended as a fast-growing screen. But with a growth rate of 3 feet a year and a mature height of 65 feet, it frequently outgrows its welcome. Don't be too eager to remove existing trees, but when adding any new trees near your pond, choose species that will stay small, and avoid willows and other species with thirsty roots.

Trees can add to your cleanup chores by dropping twigs, berries, nuts, and leaves into the pond, where this debris may decompose and change water chemistry. Be aware that some plants that otherwise make attractive windbreaks—such as yews, rhododendrons, hollies, and mountain laurels—have toxic leaves that can harm fish if allowed to accumulate. Pine needles contain tannins that can turn water brown and sicken fish. Willows put out thirsty roots that can punch through pond liners that have even tiny leaks. Again, study your desired species. Learn how wide it will eventually spread, and plant it far enough from your pond so that its branches won't end up hanging over the water.

Tree Placement. Maintain existing trees, but choose new ones carefully if they will be near your pond.

Microclimates. Wind and trees are just two of the factors that can create what are called microclimates in your garden. Your house also creates microclimates—cool and shady on the north, warm and sunny on the south, with gentle morning sun on the east, and hotter afternoon sun on the west. The same is true for outbuildings, fences, or a solid line of trees or shrubs.

A large paved area, such as a driveway or a patio, will create a hot spot. This can mean faster evaporation from a nearby pond and require more frequent watering of plants. The bottom of a slope is often a frost pocket, several degrees cooler than the top, so your pond and plants will freeze earlier and thaw later there.

If summers are short, you can extend your water-gardening season by looking for sites on your property that get the greatest sun exposure. If summers are long and hot, you can reduce evaporation and protect fish and plants by giving the water some protection from the sun at midday or in the afternoon.

Slopes and Runoff. Slopes create an array of possibilities and challenges for water gardeners. A steep slope lends itself easily to waterfalls and natural-looking rock terraces. A gentle slope presents an opportunity to create a stream. Even though nature creates ponds at the bottoms of slopes, this can be the worst place for an artificial pond. Runoff from a slope can wash dirt and debris into the pond, as well as pollutants such as lawn chemicals. Even if you don't use fertilizers or toxins in your garden, neighbors uphill may. And other substances toxic to fish can wash in from driveways and rooftops.

It's possible to divert runoff with retaining walls or ditches on either side of your pond. But there are still other problems with a slope. As previously noted, the bottom of a slope may be several degrees cooler than other parts of your yard. And the bottom of a slope is also where you are most likely to encounter problems with the water table.

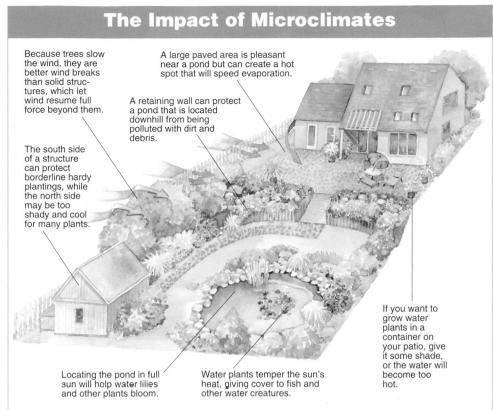

The Impact of Microclimates

Because trees slow the wind, they are better wind breaks than solid structures, which let wind resume full force beyond them.

The south side of a structure can protect borderline hardy plantings, while the north side may be too shady and cool for many plants.

A large paved area is pleasant near a pond but can create a hot spot that will speed evaporation.

A retaining wall can protect a pond that is located downhill from being polluted with dirt and debris.

If you want to grow water plants in a container on your patio, give it some shade, or the water will become too hot.

Locating the pond in full sun will help water lilies and other plants bloom.

Water plants temper the sun's heat, giving cover to fish and other water creatures.

Microclimates. Many factors have an impact on your pond's water, plants, and fish. Study your property's little idiosyncrasies to maximize success.

Shady Rest. For a small pond, a little shade reduces algae and evaporation and keeps people and pets cool.

Lush Foliage. Visit as many ponds as possible to get a feel for what you like. This one would probably excite a native plant lover.

Underground Surprises. If you dig a pond below the water table, problems may arise. Flexible pond liners can balloon up and rigid liners can heave out of the ground, or the soil around them can erode. Determine the depth of the water table under your potential pond site by digging some test holes.

These test holes will also tell you about the composition of your soil. Soil texture can vary from one area of your property to another. Good garden loam is easiest to work. Other soil types require a bit more work. Heavy clay soil is harder to excavate, whereas sandy or pebbly soil can collapse along the edges.

Rocks and a high water table may not be the only surprises you'll hit with your shovel. Hitting underground utilities can be a nasty shock—literally. Most areas now have a single agency with a memorable name such as "Miss Utility" that will come out to your home and mark any underground lines.

Convenience. While you don't want your pond on top of your electrical line, you do need access to power. You need to hook up pumps for a waterfall, aeration, or cleaning; mechanical filters; and fountains. Lighting likewise requires electricity. You should also locate your water garden near a water source because midsummer droughts, leaks, and natural evaporation will require that you occasionally top off your pond's water level.

Of secondary concern, depending on your stamina, is access to tools used to clean your pond and tend your plants, and a shed or garage to overwinter tropical water plants. It isn't much fun to lug sopping-wet lilies a long distance when autumn's first "norther" is blowing.

Size and Styles

Once you've picked a spot that's breathtaking, but not backbreaking, think about the size and style of pond that you want. Give these decisions long and careful consideration because while you may easily reshape and replant a flower bed, you'll find it difficult to reshape or move a water garden.

Your best bet is to visit as many other ponds as possible before finalizing your plans. Some water-garden suppliers have demonstration ponds, as do public gardens. Although many public water features will seem too huge and expensive to relate to your home garden, focus on the details: the overall shape and setting, the plants, and the material used for the edge and the surround. If nothing else, you will gain a sense of what you like.

Traditionally, ponds have been divided into formal and informal styles. The style you choose will guide your choice not only of pond shape but also of plants, decorations such as fountains and statues, and other materials that you use around your pond. The design guidelines for a formal style are not as flexible as those for an informal style. The style tips that follow are merely suggestions. In the end, you'll need to make the choices that please you.

Size

Most people err with a pond that is too small. A small pond in the middle of an open lawn can look lost. In a typical, sparsely planted suburban backyard, a pond up to one-third the area can be pleasingly balanced. But the more heavily your garden is planted, the more charming a tiny pond can be as an element in a busy bed or along a landscaped path. Use a rope or a hose to mark the pond outline, and live with the layout a few days.

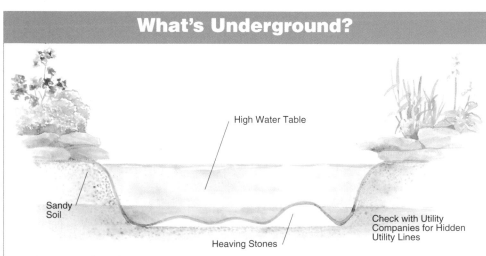

What's Underground?

High Water Table

Sandy Soil

Heaving Stones

Check with Utility Companies for Hidden Utility Lines

What's under that soil? A high water table, heaving stones, sharp hidden objects, utility lines—any one of these can cause a significant problem.

Consider 18 inches the minimum depth for an in-ground pond. The colder your climate, the deeper your pond must be to keep the roots of water lilies and other hardy water-garden perennials from freezing in winter. A local water-garden supplier or an Extension Agent can advise you on your area's frost line (the depth at which your soil freezes in the average winter). Even in relatively warm climates, koi ponds are an exception to the usual depth recommendations. Koi are large fish that need water at least 3 and preferably 4 feet deep. Ponds designed to attract wildlife should vary in depth and include some shallow ledges or a tapering beach area to invite different aquatic creatures, birds, and mammals.

Formal Styles

Generally, formal pools are geometric—square, rectangular, circular, triangular, or some combination—and have a clearly defined edge. They typically include features such as fountains or statues but rarely bridges or stepping-stones. Plantings are minimal. Surrounding plants are often those commonly used in formal gardens, such as pruned boxwood hedges, topiaries, or rose standards. But today there is a trend toward more relaxed-looking plants (especially ornamental grasses) in the landscape surrounding formal water features. Some designers believe that only formal pools are appropriate in urban gardens and even most suburban yards. Formal pools can be dug into the ground, be of a raised or semiraised style, or be sunken into a patio. Raised pools may be less of a safety hazard for small children. They are also easier to tend without bending and stooping, and they can be built with a wide edge that allows you to admire goldfish without having to drop down to your knees.

Formal water features are generally defined by their geometric shapes, above and right. They needn't be big to be elegant.

The trend today is toward more relaxed plantings, such as these mixed beds, right.

A formal water garden may be integrated into the landscape through the use of materials used in other structures.

Informal possibilities. With an informal water garden, you have the greatest design latitude and the opportunity to create something truly unique.

with fountains are not planted at all. A single dramatic tree—such as a weeping pear or a bonsai on a pedestal—or a matched pair of containers holding rosemary will complement the emphasis on hard materials.

Around the pool, consider using conifers and other plants that lend themselves to pruning. Some of the most famous formal pools are surrounded on three sides only by a clipped, U-shaped hedge. Some contemporary pools in country settings have what amounts to a "hedge" of ornamental grasses. Adjacent flower beds, when present, are often geometric in shape, like the pool, and are planted with a limited selection of species.

Within the pool, water lilies and lotuses will look beautiful if they aren't disturbed by the splashing of a fountain. Restricting yourself to water lilies and other low, horizontal plants can make the garden seem larger. But if you find this effect too static, consider adding individual clumps of ornamental grasses, a tub of cattails, or margins of irises, lilies, or daylilies. Their more vertical shapes will add visual interest.

Informal Styles

An informal pond can range from one that is a bit more playful in shape to one that mimics nature with a carefully planned mini-ecosystem of native plants and adjacent bogs. In addition to being irregular in outline, most informal water gardens are built into the ground with their edges concealed by natural-shaped stones, pebble beaches, or tall native grasses. They are unlikely to include fountains and more likely to be complemented by waterfalls or streams. You can keep plants to a minimum and employ rather traditional cultivated annuals and perennials, or you can surround the pond with so many subtropicals or wetland species that the water surface almost disappears under such a vast assortment of floaters, creepers, and waving grasses.

Informal ponds can be appropriate for many styles of homes and gardens, from old farmhouses to ultramodern designs, rich with natural woods and windows. If your home is in a natural setting of fields or woods, or if you can picture it in such a setting, it probably deserves an informal pond.

Hardscape and Ornaments. The lines of a formal pool need to be kept plain and simple. The crisp edges are built with regularly shaped materials such as bricks, machine-cut stones, tiles, or landscaping ties. If you want to create a patio or a path beside the pool, consider using a material similar to that used for the edging. Within or adjacent to a deck, the same wood decking can be used to create a pool that is formal in shape yet relaxed in feel. For benches, look to classic designs such as stone or park benches; to create shade, consider a wisteria arbor of white columns or something similarly elegant.

A fountain can also serve a practical purpose: if you have fish and don't have a waterfall, a fountain will aerate the water for them. In a small pool, though, a fountain may disturb the water too much for water lilies.

Some statues are designed to highlight water by appearing to walk on it or to chase fish. Others double as fountains by pouring or spraying water. Remember that one such arresting figure is generally enough for a pool.

Bridges and stepping-stones can work in a formal design if they are geometric. Waterfalls and streams for a formal pool are normally highly stylized with water falling in a curtain over a sheet of acrylic or down a series of stone steps.

Softscape. As for plantings in and around a formal pool, the species of plants are less important than the manner in which they are employed. Formal pools are usually planted with restraint so that the clean outline of the pool and its edging remain apparent. Some small formal pools

Hardscape and Ornaments. The edging of informal ponds is usually quarried or hand-cut stone intended to mimic nature. Similar stones may be arranged in tiers to serve as the foundation of waterfalls. Islands are sometimes included in large ponds; boulders serve that purpose in smaller ponds. Paths and surrounding areas are of natural materials such as bark, pine needles, or gravel. Architectural elements are kept to a minimum, but they might include arbors of grapevines or bent willow. Seating can be of almost any style that beckons the viewer to stop awhile and relax. For accents, possibilities could include a simple birdhouse, boulders, or sculptures. Wood is the most appropriate material for bridges. In keeping with the level of informality you choose, options range from a span of decking to weathered planks to a single fallen tree across a stream. (Flatten the undersides of the ends so that it doesn't roll, and cover the top with hardly noticeable chicken wire to provide traction for walking.) Handrails of rustic timber with bark still attached will add to the informality and safety of these choices.

Stepping-stones, like edging, should be naturally craggy rather than cut, and arranged in an uneven line. A single slab of weathered stone may do for a small pond or a narrow stream. The most informal ponds are not a place for fountains, except those that bubble just above the surface like a natural spring. A simple spray or geyser is good for slightly more formal ponds.

Arrangement. When hardscaping, combine natural elements, such as stone slabs and boulders, with ornaments. Arrange elements in tiers.

Continuity. Even around the most informal pond, use restraint in varying plant species, and group them in bold masses.

Imitating Nature. Depending upon its design, an informal water site may simply mimic the beauty of nature or elevate it to a very complex level that duplicates an ecosystem.

Softscape. Even though there are fewer guidelines for planting informal water gardens than for formal pools, resist the urge to plant one of every variety you can get your hands on. Strive for a minimum of three plants of each variety. An uneven number of plants in clusters or masses will keep your design from looking stiff and formal. The edges of your planting areas should be big bold curves, not little squiggles or straight lines.

In addition to taking design cues from your home's architecture, you might want to choose a planting style that is regionally appropriate both in aesthetics and plant materials. For example, rock gardens often become an adjunct to water features through serendipity, when gardeners with a mound of leftover dirt or rocks put two and two together. Such gardens look right at home in arid mountain climates, because many traditional rock-garden plants flourish in the bright sun and dry climate there. If you live surrounded by deciduous woodlands, fill your rock garden with plants that grow naturally in this environment. Good bets include ferns, native ground covers, or ornamentals such as creeping bellflower that droop gracefully over embankments.

If you live in the subtropics, an appealing option is to strive for the jungle look, cramming your pond with tropical water lilies, parrot's-feather, and giant papyrus, and planting the surrounding area with huge-leaved green taro, hibiscus, and giant chain fern. But if you have a Zone 7 garden with a warmer Zone 9 spirit, capture a tropical feel with lush-leaved perennials such as ligularia and hosta, evergreen shrubs such as acuba, and a hardier species of papyrus.

Wildlife Gardens

Sometimes style will be dictated by the goal of the water feature. Many people create ponds for the express purpose of attracting wildlife, and such ponds are inherently informal. If you have a closely mowed lawn and carefully cultivated perimeter beds, you may not have much luck attracting wildlife with the pond in the middle of your yard, no matter how informal or lushly planted it may be. Consider relaxing your yard-keeping standards a bit and placing your pond against a small woodlot, a shrub border, or even a woodpile to provide cover so small creatures feel safe.

A wildlife pond should create as diverse a habitat as possible, with some deep-water areas and some shallow areas, including a gradually sloping pebble beach for wading and washing. The goal is to provide the things natural creatures need, including food and shelter. A diversity of shrubs and dense plantings, especially grasses, supplies places to hide as well as things to eat: berries from the shrubs, seeds from the grasses, and insects that lurk in the foliage. The pond shouldn't advertise human presence too loudly, although a big flat stone will give the gardener, as well as turtles and butterflies, an inviting place to sun.

Fun for All. All children love being around water. A shallow, natural-style pond can be both educational and safe.

Some flowering aquatic plants grow well in shallow containers, top.

Be sure to select a site that you will see often because a water-filled container isn't easy to move, right.

Situate a container garden so that it gets some shade during the day.

Water Gardens in Containers

One of the easiest ways to try your hand at water gardening is to create a miniature pond in a container. You can use something as elegant as a ceramic planter or as rustic as an old horse trough, kettle, or whiskey half barrel. Choose a container at least 18 inches in diameter—24 inches can be even better.

Locate your container garden where you can enjoy it often, such as on a deck or a patio. Because it will overheat more quickly than a pond in the ground, situate the container so that it gets some shade during the hottest part of the day. It will also need frequent topping off and cleaning, so consider how you will drain the container and refill it; a spot within reach of a hose works best. Keep in mind that the planter will be heavy when filled.

Add a liner to your container to keep it from rusting or leaking and to prevent any toxins it might contain from harming plants or fish. There are now fiberglass shells made especially for half barrels. For other containers, use a piece of PVC liner.

Although you shouldn't cram the container with plants, it's possible to enjoy a half-dozen species in even a small one. In Chapter 10, you'll find many water lilies that adapt to tub gardens. Try to include an upright plant or two, as well as one that will hang gracefully over the side. If the container is too deep for a marginal species, grow one in a pot set on one or more bricks.

A few small goldfish or mosquito fish will help keep your mini-pond free of mosquito larvae. Unless you live in a warm-winter climate or can sink the container into the ground for the winter, you'll need to transfer the fish to an indoor aquarium for a few months each year. Also plan on replacing most of the plants. If you have a sunroom with a tile floor, you may be able to move the whole display indoors. (In the case of a particularly large container, you may want to have a contractor do an inspection and verify that your floor will support its weight when filled with water.)

pond materials

BEFORE INSTALLING A POND you must decide on some preliminary issues. Will you use a flexible or pre-formed pond liner? What other materials are available? How will you configure the pond? How will you create the pond's edging? Do you need a site plan before you begin? These subjects and more are covered in the following pages.

Liners

You can't expect to simply dig a hole in the ground and have it hold water. You'll need to provide a watertight foundation. Most ponds today are built using flexible liners or preformed shells. Either material can be used to create a formal pool or an informal pond. You'll also need to provide an edging to mask the rim of the liner; edging can be a visual asset by clearly delineating a formal pool or helping an informal pond blend into the landscape.

Flexible Pond Liners

Although they're called flexible because of their physical malleability, the big selling point of these liners is their design flexibility. From a small and shallow splash pool for toddlers to a raised koi pond for fish hobbyists, from a multi-acre fishing hole to a winding creek, you can make a flexible liner adapt to your design. Flexible liners are also relatively inexpensive and easy for do-it-yourselfers to install. You lay the liner in the hole, fill the pond with water, trim the liner, and install the edging.

Polyethylene liners resemble the black plastic sheeting sold in hardware stores, but they're much thicker. Polyethylene sheeting isn't particularly durable, though, so don't use it for a pond unless you want just a small, temporary one with which to try your hand at water gardening for a couple of years. You can, however, use it successfully for a wetland or bog garden, because in such situations it doesn't need to be watertight.

Liners made especially for ponds are either PVC (polyvinyl chloride) or synthetic rubber—either butyl rubber or EPDM (ethylene propylene diene monomer). English gardening books usually talk about butyl, which is made only in Sweden, but EPDM is more readily available in North America. Be sure you get a liner made for ponds; EPDM rubber sheeting that is intended for use on roofs and other purposes can contain toxins harmful to plants and fish.

Naturally, the best liners cost more. Rubber liners last longer than the best of the less-expensive PVC liners because they are stretchable and more resistant to ultraviolet light. Thicker liners of any type generally last longer, too. Butyl or EPDM rubber liners are available in thicknesses from 30 to 45 mil and will typically last from 20 to 30 years. PVC liners are available in thicknesses from 20 to 32 mil. At the bottom end of the scale, a 20-mil-thick PVC liner can be expected to last between 5 and 7 years;

a 32-mil-thick PVC liner will last between 10 and 15 years.

Flexible pond liners come in stock sizes ranging from about 5 x 5 feet to 30 x 50 feet. Some manufacturers offer custom sizes, which are priced by the square foot. By joining the edges of the sheets with seam sealer, you can create any size or shape you want.

Because flexible liners are susceptible to punctures from rocks, gravel, broken tree roots, or other sharp objects, you should cushion the liner with an underlayment of some kind. An underlayment is a lot like a carpet pad, and in fact, carpet pad is one possible choice. Other options include 2 to 3 inches of sand, fiberglass insulation material, or layers of newspaper. However, sand won't pack well onto steep sidewalls, and it can be heavy to transport. The problem with newspapers is that they tend to deteriorate over time. (Even carpet padding deteriorates eventually.) So most water-garden suppliers offer a tough, flexible underlayment material sold under various brand names that is specifically designed for use with pond liners. You can also buy liners with underlayment material bonded to the liner material.

If your soil is especially rocky, full of roots, or subject to excessive shifting during winter months, you should install both a layer of sand and underlayment fabric. If the soil is stable, fine grained, and rock free, however, the underlayment really isn't needed (unless you expect heavy traffic from wading children or large, rambunctious pets).

Pond Construction. With careful planning and by selecting the proper materials, you can build a waterfall and pond like this one. If you're hesitant about your skills or the time involved, consult a specialist who will work with your ideas and within your budget.

Preformed Pond Shells

Pond shells may be made of rigid or semirigid materials that are premolded to a specific shape and are easy to install yourself. Although they come in an array of sizes, shapes, and depths, they won't give you the design choices that a flexible liner does. They are generally more expensive for their size but are also more durable and puncture-proof. Shells can last from 5 to 50 years, depending on their composition, thickness, quality, and installation conditions. The thickest shells (¼ inch or more) can be installed aboveground with little support around the sides, provided the bottom rests on a firm and level base.

Your first choice should be rigid fiberglass, which is durable and easy to repair. Although it may discolor if exposed to sunlight, it should last 10 to 30 years. Semirigid plastic shells are more difficult to repair, aren't sturdy enough to be used aboveground, and become brittle. Their life span is less than 10 years. Make sure whatever you buy is resistant to ultraviolet radiation.

Most manufacturers offer between 10 and 15 pond-shell designs. Depths range from 9 to 18 inches. If you want to raise water lilies, the shell should be a minimum of 18 inches deep. Unless you live in a subtropical climate, shallower ponds are likely to freeze solid in winter, so you'll need to bring fish indoors. Capacities range from about 30 to 500 gallons. Keep in mind that the shell will look larger when out of the ground than when installed. Decide the dimensions you want ahead of time, and don't be concerned if the shell looks too large in the store.

Many preformed shells have ledges partway down the sides for shallow-water (marginal) plants. Make sure these are at least 9 inches wide, though, or they won't be practical. A few shell models also have depressions around the perimeter for wetland plants. Some shells have integrated premolded waterfall lips; you can also buy separate premolded waterfall courses.

The perimeter of a preformed pond can be more difficult to disguise with edging than that of a liner pond. It tends to be more obvious and offers less "give" to heavy rocks, as well as less support. Burying a line of concrete blocks around the outside of the perimeter will help hold the rim vertical against the weight of rocks on top and the weight of water inside the pond.

Other Options

Concrete Ponds. Years ago, practically all garden ponds were made of poured concrete, concrete block, or a combination of the two. But the popularity of these materials waned with the advent of flexible pond liners and premolded pond shells, which are easier to install and can even be dug up and moved if you relocate. Not only does pouring a concrete pond require a great deal of skill and backbreaking work, it is also more expensive than other options, even if you do the work. A concrete pond can last a lifetime if properly installed but will crack and leak almost immediately if it is not. Once a crack opens, there's usually no way to permanently repair it. The best fix is to cover the concrete with a flexible pond liner.

Pond Shell Options

Pond with Waterfall Lip   **Pond with Full Shelf**

Deep Pond with Partial Shelf   **Pond with Stream**

These plastic or fiberglass preformed pond foundations come in many different shapes that make design decisions for you. They are easy to install but limited in depth and overall size.

Choosing Materials

A Guide to Foundations. You need to decide between a flexible liner and a preformed shell. Each offers benefits and drawbacks. Whichever you choose, specify quality material for durability.

MATERIAL	ADVANTAGES	DISADVANTAGES
Flexible Liner	■ Unlimited shapes, sizes ■ Less expensive than preformed shell ■ Inexpensive to ship ■ Folds small enough to transport in car ■ Easy to customize for wetland, marginal plants ■ Easier to conceal edges	■ Less durable ■ Punctures easily ■ Degrades in sunlight ■ Any exposed material must be covered
Preformed Shell	■ Lasts longer ■ Resists punctures ■ Small units easy to install ■ Relatively quick installation ■ Poses no design concerns ■ Easier to clean	■ Limited sizes, shapes ■ Hard to customize ■ More expensive than flexible liner ■ Hard to conceal edges ■ Needs to be perfectly level ■ Requires firm foundation to prevent buckling

If you decide to use concrete, have the pond installed by a masonry contractor familiar with this sort of construction in your particular climate (and familiar with local building codes). In cold climates, the concrete shell must be at least 6 inches thick and adequately reinforced with ½-inch (No. 2) reinforcing bar ("rebar") or wire mesh to ensure that the pond will survive alternate freezing and thawing. In milder climates, the shell should still be 3 to 4 inches thick.

New concrete can leach lime into the pond water, so you must neutralize the lime with acidic chemicals—or seal the concrete with a coat of paint—before adding fish and plants to the pond. You can paint concrete with a rubber-based pool paint to create various effects: use earth tones for a natural look, white or blue for a more formal appearance, or dark colors for a "bottomless" look.

Clay and Bentonite. To create the most natural wildlife or farm ponds, where edging is minimal and punctures unheard of, it's possible to construct a clay-bottomed pond. For very large ponds, where handling a liner becomes unwieldy, this is often the preferred approach. Where the soil is already heavy clay, you can make the pond bottom watertight by stomping it, pounding it with a post, or renting a special tool (a tamper) to compact it. You can also make the soil more watertight by mixing in bentonite, a powdered clay made from volcanic ash. In addition, you can buy flexible liners made of bentonite granules sandwiched between layers of landscape fabric; you may be able to order them through your water-gardening supplier under the brand name Bentomat or Bentofix. The bentonite swells when it gets wet and forms a tight seal. The downside of a clay pond is that the bottom and sides will crack if allowed to go dry, and it's easily damaged by roots or tunneling animals.

Pond Kits. Some manufacturers offer complete pond kits. These include a rigid shell or flexible liner with a matched pump, filter, and in some cases a fountainhead or self-contained waterfall, planting containers, and pond-treatment chemicals for the initial start-up—you just add the plants and any fish you may want. If you find a design you like, the kits are much easier to install than separate components. But you must bring electrical power to the pond location to operate the pump and lighting affects, and you must still excavate, which is often the most difficult part of building a pond. Such kits are usually limited to smaller ponds, however.

Lawn Edging

A turf edging can give a pond a clean, open look and easy access for maintenance, but can be difficult to maintain.

Pebble Beach

A gradual slope with a pebble bottom makes an ideal edging for a wildlife pond. Birds and other animals can easily bathe, drink, and wash their food.

Edging Options

Pond edgings are typically rock, other masonry materials, or wood. The edging serves to hide the rim, visually define the pond perimeter, and keep surrounding soil from washing into the water. The material you choose can complement nearby landscape or architectural features; the edging for a formal pond might also be decorative in its own right. As an alternative, the edging can blend into the surroundings, as is the case with an informal pond edged with lawn or native stone. Plan for the edging (also called coping) to overhang the pond by a few inches so that it hides the liner.

At least one section of the edging should be wide and flat enough to allow easy access to the pond for maintenance tasks. (An overhang of a deck or patio could also serve this purpose.) Because stepping on edging could dislodge it, be sure that the area intended for maintenance access is secure; you may wish to mortar at least a portion. Design the edging so that it rises slightly above the surrounding ground to direct runoff away from the pond.

Solid Edging. Formal pools usually have the same edging all the way around, typically poured concrete, brick, pavers, patio tiles, or cut stone. The most common edging for an informal pond is one line of natural stones, either boulders or flagstones. But you may stack flagstones in several vertical layers or arrange boulders and round stones several feet from the pond, decreasing in size as they get closer to the water. Or you can edge an informal pond with a mix of plantings and different types of stone.

Lawn Edging. Lawn grass can make a handsome edging for a water garden, but you'll have to trim it by hand, taking care not to drop grass clippings in the water because the high nitrogen content will disturb the chemical balance of the pond. Still, you might want to create a short edge of lawn so that you can get near the water for maintenance or for observing fish. You can make a solid edge for a lawn by embedding stones or bricks in mortar on a ledge along the edge of the pond and bringing sod to the edge on a thin layer of topsoil.

Pebble Beach. For a wildlife pond, a pebble beach is a popular edging option because it allows birds and mammals to bathe or to wash their food in the shallow water. To create a beach, dig a gradual slope into your pond on one side and surface it with pebbles. Unless you want pebbles on the bottom of your pond—which is not advisable because the plant debris that gets trapped between them makes the pond hard to clean—you need to create a lip, or stone step, 4 to 6 inches under the water surface to keep the pebbles from rolling into the pond. (Mortar is another option, but it will have to be neutralized with vinegar or acid. See Step 6 on pages 32–33.) The beach will look more natural if you gradually decrease the size of the pebbles as they get nearer the pond. Lay them down thickly enough so that the liner doesn't show through; some coarse sand may help fill the gaps. If your pond is small, keep the beach area small, or the high percentage of shallow water will cause excessive algae buildup.

Wood Edging. In the unlikely event that you use wood as an edging material, make sure it's labeled for marine or seawall use. Avoid pressure-treated wood because it is treated with chemicals that are toxic to fish and plants.

Buying Rocks for Your Pond

Well-chosen and appropriately placed rocks often mark the difference between an obviously amateur pond and one that looks professionally installed. Most stone dealers will sell natural stone for informal ponds as well as stones machine-cut in geometric shapes appropriate for edging a formal pool. If you can possibly afford and handle them, large boulders will look better than small stones. Buy the largest stones you can manage easily, but also look for smaller stones of the same type. These can help fill gaps between the bigger rocks and create a transition between them and the pond.

A landscape designer, a local nursery, or your water-garden dealer may be able to suggest a local quarry with a good selection and helpful service for do-it-yourselfers. Otherwise, telephone first with questions to sample the staff's patience and expertise. A quarry will offer local stone, which will look more appropriate in your landscape than exotic imports. Ask for local stone if you visit a dealer rather than a quarry.

If possible, visit a couple of quarries or dealers to get an idea of what's available. If you call first, you may get a sense of which ones will be most helpful. A visit to a good rock quarry can be a fun experience. You can find rocks with holes for waterfalls, flat rocks perfect for the waterfall lip, rocks with natural depressions for a Japanese basin, and moss-covered rocks to give your pond an instant weathered look. Rock is usually described as either permeable (allowing water to penetrate) or impermeable. Permeable rock such as sandstone will weather quickly and develop a natural-looking roundness; it provides a good home for moss and comes in a variety of colors. Slate has a handsome sheen when wet. Avoid limestone, as it will turn the pond water too alkaline. Granite is an impermeable stone that, while handsome, is more suited to a formal pool. It is durable but difficult to cut.

This informal pond is surrounded by natural stone and lawn, making maintenance easier.

The owner of this pond installed a preformed shell that was deep enough for growing water lilies.

Designing the Pond Configuration

A formal reflecting pool with no plants or fish needs to be only 12 inches deep. Other ponds should be at least 18 to 24 inches deep, considered the optimum for growing water lilies and other aquatic plants and sufficient for nearly all types of fish except koi. Keep in mind, though, that ponds less than 18 inches deep heat up and cool off quicker than large, deep ones.

Except in very cold climates (Zone 3), a depth of 24 inches is sufficient to prevent the pond from freezing to the bottom and killing fish or damaging the pond shell. If you live in an area with harsh winters, contact local pond builders for recommended depths.

A pond for Japanese koi needs to be at least 3 feet deep, preferably 4 feet, so that these somewhat demanding fish get room to grow and can escape summer heat.

Shallow and Sloping Areas. You may want to build in some special shallow areas for marginal plants, which need water depths of a foot or less. You can design either separate planting beds or shelves around the pond perimeter, although many people find it easier and more flexible to keep their pond a uniform depth and raise containerized plants to their recommended depths on bricks or blocks of some kind. (See illustration below for both concepts). Plastic milk crates are a popular option because they are lightweight and easy to handle.

In general, your pond will look best and hold more water if it has steeply sloping sides—about 20 degrees off vertical. Clay ponds should have a shallow bowl shape to make the edges less prone to cracking or crumbling if they dry out. Wildlife ponds often have one side that is a shallow pebble beach so that birds and other creatures have an inviting place to wade.

Finally, don't make your pond's bottom perfectly flat. Instead, you should slope it slightly toward a sump hole, which will trap dirt and debris and ease cleaning. You can also use this sump area as a drain location or as a place for a submersible pump to improve water circulation. You will need to elevate the pump on a brick (or by other means) to keep it above sediment in the sump bottom, so dig your hole deep enough to accommodate both pump and brick.

The Pond Bottom

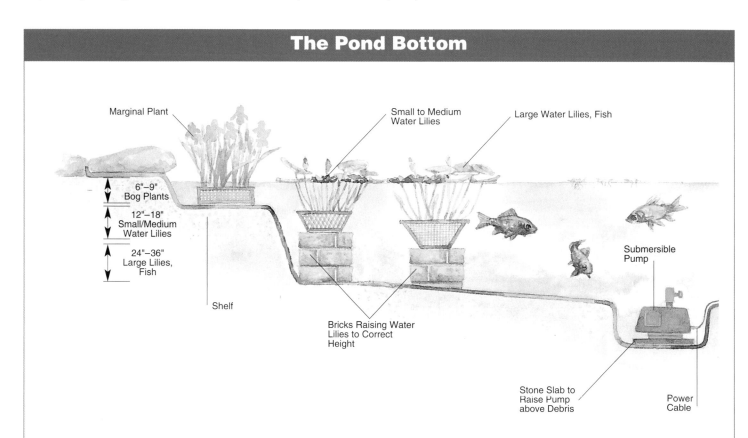

Marginal Plant

Small to Medium Water Lilies

Large Water Lilies, Fish

6"–9" Bog Plants

12"–18" Small/Medium Water Lilies

24"–36" Large Lilies, Fish

Shelf

Bricks Raising Water Lilies to Correct Height

Submersible Pump

Stone Slab to Raise Pump above Debris

Power Cable

Before you begin digging your pond, think about the needs of its future inhabitants. Water lilies require a minimum depth of 18 inches. Koi and other large fish need ponds 3 feet deep. If you want to have marginal plants, such as grass, sedges, arrowhead, and pickerel weed, you will have to accommodate them in water depths ranging anywhere from an inch or two to a foot, either by building shelves or raising them on bricks or plastic baskets. Sloping the bottom toward the sump hole will make pond cleaning much easier.

Making a Site Plan

If you've selected a site for your pond and you plan to leave the rest of the yard pretty much as it is, a site plan isn't necessary. But sometimes a pond is part of a larger landscaping project. In that case, it's a good idea to develop a site plan. This plan can also be submitted to your local building department for approval, if that is required. Local building codes are likely to have requirements relating to setbacks and safety barriers to protect young children. Check before you begin.

To make the site plan, you'll need some graph paper for a base map and some tracing paper for overlays. If you have the original site survey map (plat) or site plan for your property, this could serve as your base map. If you don't have the original map, use a measuring tape to help determine the size of the lot and to locate existing features such as the house, decks, outbuildings, and trees.

1 **Mark the property lines.** On the graph paper, mark your property lines (a scale of ⅛ inch = 1 foot is standard). If only a portion of the property will be affected, such as the backyard, you don't need to include the entire lot. Indicate north, south, east, and west. Also mark the directions of prevailing summer and winter winds. (Ask your local Cooperative Extension Service if you're not sure.) Check with the building department to see how far the pond or any added structures must be set back from lot boundaries; mark these setbacks as dotted lines.

Locate existing structures. Starting from a front corner of the house, measure the house dimensions, and transfer them to the plan. Again, if only one area will be affected, you need only show the part of the house that faces it. Include the locations of exterior doors and windows on the wall facing the pond site. Measure and mark the locations of your garage, storage shed, and any other detached buildings and permanent structures, including patios, decks, fences, and paved walks. Show any underground or overhead fixtures, such as utility lines and septic systems. Utility companies will mark these for you.

2 **Locate plantings.** Mark the locations of existing trees, shrubs, and other major plantings; specify which are to be kept and which need to be removed or relocated. If applicable, note where shade is cast by trees, fences, or other structures near the pond site. Remember to factor in growth of any immature trees and large shrubs.

Locate the pond on overlays. On a tracing-paper overlay, draw in the exact size and location of the proposed pond. Include edging materials and other proposed pond features, such as a waterfall, walks, planting beds, and fountains. Show the path of new utility lines to the pond. Use as many overlay sheets as you need.

Once you've finalized the design, make a neat tracing. Attach this overlay to the base map. Make a photocopy for your files, give another one to building officials, and keep at least two more copies for use during the project.

Tools & Materials

- Graph paper (⅛-inch grid)
- Tracing paper, several sheets
- 50-foot measuring tape
- Pencil ■ Ruler
- Site survey map (plat), if available

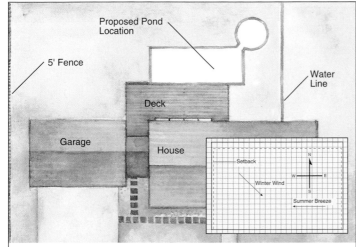

1 Measure the dimensions of the house and other structures on the property; then transfer them to your plan.

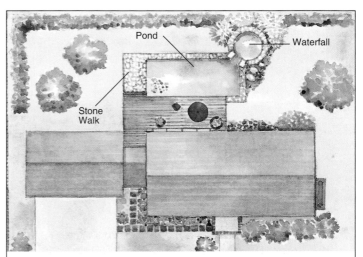

2 Mark locations of existing plantings; then draw in the pond and other new features on a tracing paper overlay.

pond foundations

WHEN BUILDING A POND, just as when building a house, laying the foundation is the most important step. It marks the end of dreaming and planning and the beginning of years of enjoyment and pleasure.

Special Sites

Most people choose a flat site on which to build a water feature. This is the simplest option for home gardeners building their first pond. The bottom of a slope is definitely not the best choice. Although nature places ponds in low-lying areas, the lowest place in your garden may be the worst spot for an artificial pond for several reasons: it will catch runoff that may be full of harmful pesticides and other toxins and will definitely contain soil and organic debris; it may be colder than the rest of your landscape; and it may be too close to the water table, greatly increasing the likelihood that groundwater could bubble up under a liner or heave a pond shell out of the ground.

Slopes. A hillside can lend itself to some creative possibilities for waterfalls and streams. On some properties, a slope may be the only choice. If that is the case for you, you'll need to build a retaining wall for the pond. You can do this with soil, using the "cut-and-fill" method. Use subsoil excavated from your pond to build a mound on the downhill side, cover it with topsoil you've removed from the area, and landscape it with plants and rocks.

You can also build a brick or concrete retaining wall on one or both sides of the pond. A wall on the uphill side can be designed so it's almost invisible aboveground. It will help prevent that slope from eroding, and its top edge can keep soil and other matter from washing into the pond. A wall on the downhill side will provide additional support for your liner or shell and the weight of the water it contains, but depending on your slope, it may be visible from below and could obstruct your view of the pond. If you build this wall of stone, you may be able to turn it into an attractive rock garden to complement an informal pond. For a formal pool you can use brick and turn it into a raised bed for growing flowers or ornamental grasses.

If your property has a high water table, your best solution is to plan on a raised or at least a semiraised pond. You may be able to deal with seasonally poor drainage by installing gravel-filled trenches to divert water around the pond and into a dry well. Such a trench will also be helpful on the uphill side of a slope to catch runoff before it reaches the level of the pond. A more attractive option is to install a wetland garden on the uphill side of the pond to catch runoff.

Taking advantage of terrain. Inclines lend themselves readily to lush waterfalls and handsome rock terraces.

Installing a Flexible Liner

Flexible pond liners of PVC plastic or rubber are by far the most popular options for pond foundations. They are both relatively inexpensive (compared to preformed shells) and easy to install, and they provide unlimited creative opportunities in pond size and shape. It's also easy to load a roll of flexible liner into your car's rear seat or trunk. Most flexible liners are black, which gives ponds the illusion of additional depth. You may occasionally see other colors. The liners come in a variety of stock sizes, with larger sizes available as special orders. Some garden suppliers carry large rolls of liner material in standard widths. You simply pull the length you need off the roll. If you don't have a well-stocked supplier within easy driving distance, consider ordering the liner by mail-order or on-line. Most mail-order suppliers and Web sites have knowledgeable, helpful staff.

Estimating the Size to Buy

Quality liner material is not inexpensive. Nor will you enjoy calling in your helpers and digging the hole, only to find that you don't have enough liner to fill it. Water-garden expert and supplier Charles Thomas recommends that anyone installing a water garden for the first time should add a foot to the calculations in both directions. (See step 2.) Redo your math a couple of times, and then have someone recheck your figures.

1 **Outline the Shape.** After clearing the site of plantings and other obstructions, outline the pond shape on the ground. For irregularly-shaped ponds, use a rope or garden hose to mark the pond perimeter **(A).** For squares or rectangles, use batter boards, string, and a framing square to make sure all corners meet exactly at a 90-degree angle **(B).** For circular ponds, make a simple "compass" with a stake, sturdy twine or rope, and a sharpened stick, screwdriver, or other pointed object. Drive the stake in the center of your pond area, attach a rope the length of its radius, and use the sharp stick or screwdriver tied to the other end to mark the pond's

Tools & Materials

- Rope and stake (for circular ponds), garden hose (for irregular ponds), or batter boards and string (for rectangular ponds)
- Framing square (for square or rectangular ponds)
- Sharpened stick (for circular ponds)
- Flour, powdered gypsum, or nontoxic spray paint (for marking outlines)
- Measuring tape and calculator

1a For a pond that contains curves, use a garden hose to outline the perimeter.

1b Ponds with square corners require the use of batter boards for precise angles.

1c For circular ponds, create a compass using a wooden stake, twine, and spray paint.

outside edge. Go over the marked line with flour, powdered gypsum, or nontoxic spray paint to make it more visible **(C).**

2 Calculate Liner Size. Measure the overall width and length of the pond; then determine the smallest rectangle that would enclose the pond area. To allow for pond depth, decide on the maximum depth of the pond, double it, and add this figure to the width and length of the rectangle. To allow for overlap around the edges, add 24 inches to the width and length of the liner. This will provide 12 inches of overlap around the pond rim once the liner is installed. It is obviously best to overestimate when calculating the liner size you'll need, particularly if the shape of the pond is irregular. (See "Formula for Liner Size," below.)

Note that for irregularly shaped ponds, you may need to trim excess liner material to provide an even overlap around the entire pond. If you are creating one or more wetland gardens alongside the pond, you may be able to use the excess for that purpose. Be sure to add extra liner to your calculations if it appears that you will not have enough for a desired wetland.

Lined In-Ground Pond

Installing a flexible liner in the ground requires four basic steps: digging the hole, laying down the liner, filling the pond with water, and adding stones or other edging around the pond perimeter. Some sites and designs may require a few additional steps. If you plan to install statuary, read about footings on page 62 before you begin your pond.

Formula for Liner Size

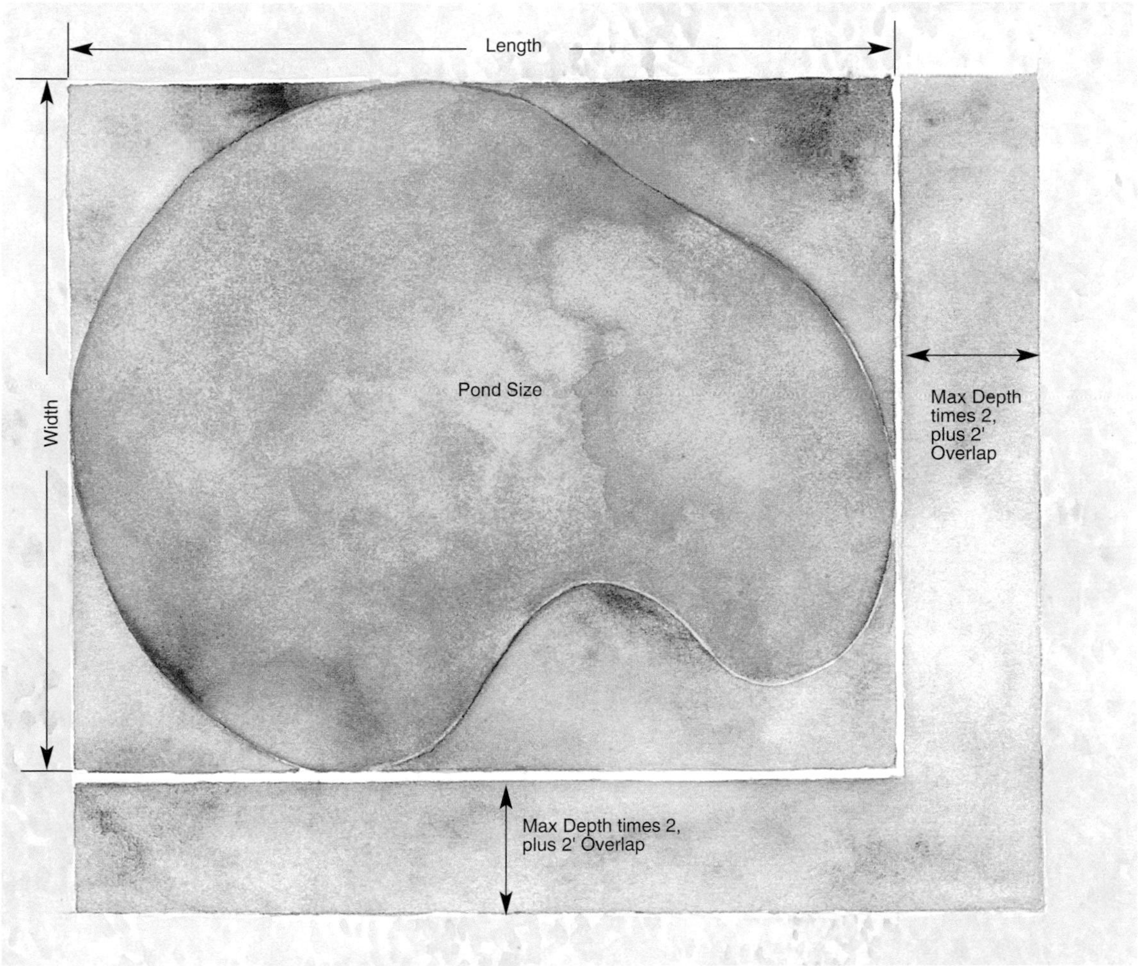

Length

Width

Pond Size

Max Depth times 2, plus 2' Overlap

Max Depth times 2, plus 2' Overlap

Example:
The pond is 24 inches deep and fits inside a 10x12-foot rectangle. To figure liner width, add 10 feet (the width), plus 4 feet (the depth, doubled), plus 2 feet (for overlap), for a total of 16 feet. To figure liner length, add 12 feet (the length), plus 4 feet (the depth, doubled), plus 2 feet (for overlap), for a total of 18 feet. You would therefore need a 16x18-foot liner for a 10x12-foot pond.

Liner Width = Pond Width + 2x Depth + 2-foot overlap

Liner Length = Pond Length + 2x Depth + 2-foot overlap

Constructing a Lined In-Ground Pond

1 Dig the Hole. If you've located the pond in a lawn area, use a flat shovel to remove patches or strips of sod within the pond outline and about 6 to 12 inches beyond the perimeter. You may be able to reuse the sod to patch your lawn or, if you're creating a wetland garden, as a divider between pond and wetland. If you can reuse it, roll it up and store it in a shady spot. Otherwise, lay the sod upside down in your compost bin. You may also dig optional shallow shelves around the pond perimeter to provide a place for containers of shallow-water (marginal) plants. Because these shelves do have some drawbacks, many water gardeners omit them, instead growing shallow-water plants by raising them on bricks or by other means.

Typically, these shelves are about 12 to 16 inches wide and 9 to 12 inches below the top edge of the excavation. Excavate the entire pond area to the depth of the shelf; then use a tamper to compact the soil firmly in the shelf area. (Hand and power tampers are available at tool-rental shops, or you can make a tamper by nailing a scrap of 2x6 to the end of a long 2x4.) Use a straight board and a spirit level to make sure the shelf is level. Then excavate the rest of the pond down to the maximum depth. Start by digging around the pond perimeter (or, if you built shelves, the shelf perimeter) to the depth of the shovel blade (9 to 12 inches). Then remove all dirt within the pond area, by layers, to the final depth. Check the depth frequently by measuring from the bottom of the hole to the top of a long 2x4 or 2x6 placed across the pond. (If your pond is too wide for any board you have on hand, rest a board on a stake in the middle of the hole.) The sides of the pond should slope in about 20 degrees from vertical; in loose or sandy soil, make the slope closer to 45 degrees. Slope the bottom of the excavation about ½ to 1 inch per foot toward the center or one end; at the lowest point, dig a shallow (6- to 8-inch deep) sump hole to facilitate draining the pond for future cleaning.

2 Cut a Ledge for the Edging Materials. With a flat-blade shovel, cut a ledge around the pond rim to provide a flat, level surface on which to install the edging materials. Depending on the materials you are using, this should generally be about 12 to 15 inches wide and deep

Terrain

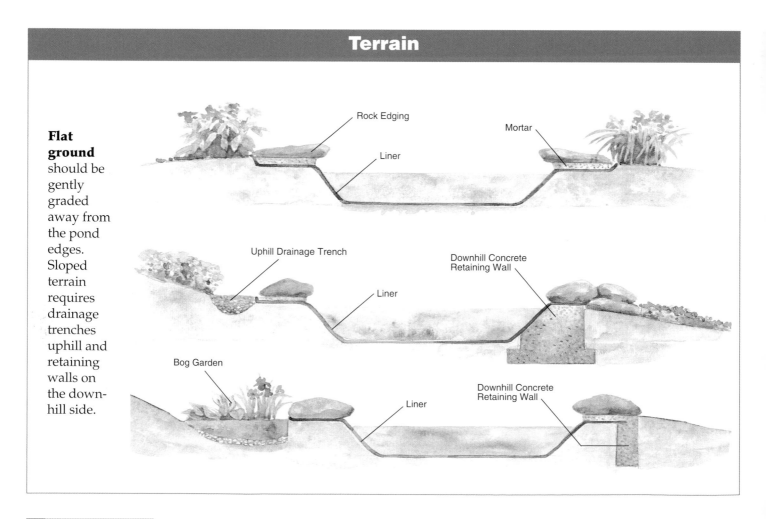

Flat ground should be gently graded away from the pond edges. Sloped terrain requires drainage trenches uphill and retaining walls on the downhill side.

Rock Edging
Mortar
Liner
Uphill Drainage Trench
Downhill Concrete Retaining Wall
Liner
Bog Garden
Downhill Concrete Retaining Wall
Liner

enough to accommodate the combined thickness of the edging and any underlayment. If you will be mortaring the stones in place, include an extra 2 to 3 inches for the mortar bed. You want the top of your finished edging to be at least 1 inch above the surrounding terrain to prevent runoff from entering the pond. You also want your edging to overhang the pond edge by a few inches to help hide the liner and to protect it from the sun.

If you'll be installing a statuary fountain that weighs more than 100 pounds, you need to install a 4-inch-thick concrete footing for it before you lay the liner.

3 Make Sure the Pond Edges are Level. If the edge of the pond has any high or low spots, they will be obvious once the pond is filled with water. The lining will show, or pond water will overflow the edging. To check for level before adding water, use the same board you used to measure hole depth. Place a level on top of the board, and then move the board to various points across the length and width of the pond while checking the level. If necessary, cut down high spots on the ledge or build up low ones until the entire pond rim is level. Carefully inspect the excavation for any sharp stones or projecting roots, and remove them. Unless you have purchased a liner with a built-in underlayment, you need to give your liner additional protection against punctures on the bottom and sides. This can be achieved with pond underlayment from your supplier, a 2- to 3-inch cushion of damp sand, old carpet, or a 1-inch layer of newspapers. Also pack damp sand or soil into any voids in the sidewalls and bottom, such as where large rocks were removed. If your soil is mostly sand and your liner is heavy, you may be able to omit underlayment on the bottom, but you should use some on the sides to reduce erosion.

Tools & Materials

- Measuring tape, spirit level, tamper
- Flexible liner
- Shovels (flat shovel works best for removing sod; rounded shovel works best for digging)
- Wheelbarrow (for moving excavated soil)
- Straight boards (for checking level)
- Underlayment fabric or old newspapers, carpet, or damp sand
- Stones for temporary liner weights
- Heavy-duty scissors or utility knife
- Very long nails (20d)
- Edging materials
- Mortar and mixing equipment, vinegar, muriatic acid, or commercial concrete-curing agent (optional, for edging)

1 Use a flat shovel to remove patches or strips of sod within the pond.

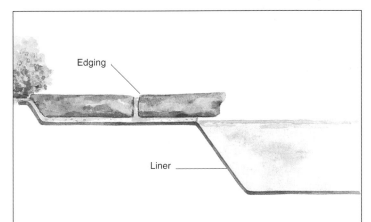

Edging

Liner

2 With a flat-blade shovel, cut a ledge around the pond rim.

3 Check for level. If there are any high or low spots, they will be obvious once the pond is filled.

(continued on page 32)

(continued from page 31)

4 Position the Liner. Pick a warm, sunny day to install the liner. It should be warm enough for you to go shoeless, or you'll need footgear that will keep your feet dry but not damage the liner. To make the liner more flexible and easier to handle, unroll or unfold it and let it warm a few minutes in the sun. Heat will build up quickly underneath it and kill a lawn, so spread it on sun-warmed pavement if possible. Avoid dragging the liner across the ground, as this may cause a puncture. With a helper, drape the liner loosely into the excavation, leaving an even overlap on all sides. After it's centered, weigh down the edges with concrete blocks, bricks, or stones. Once the liner is in place, fill the pond with water.

5 Fit and Fill the Liner. As the pond fills with water, adjust the liner to conform to the sides of the pond; smooth out as many creases and wrinkles as possible.

Large creases at tight corners can be stretched out and pleated to make them less noticeable. As the pond fills, periodically ease off the stone weights to avoid overstretching the liner. When the pond is full, trim off excess lining with a heavy pair of scissors or a utility knife. Leave enough liner around the pond rim to extend underneath and a few inches behind the first course of edging stones, and to extend into any wetland areas that you have planned. To keep the liner in place while you add edging, push large nails or spikes through the liner into the ground every foot or so around the pond rim.

6 Add Edging Materials. The simplest and most popular way to edge an informal pond is to lay a single line of natural stones around the perimeter. Make several trial arrangements until you find one that looks most natural and leaves the smallest gap between stones. (You may

4 Drape the liner loosely in the excavated area. The overlap should be even on all sides.

5 As you begin filling the pond, smooth out any wrinkles, and adjust the liner as necessary.

6 Install edging stones on top of an additional layer of liner material.

7 Place perimeter plantings between edging material or in pots.

be able to reshape some stones with a chisel.) Large, heavy stones can be installed without mortar, especially where there won't be any foot traffic, but position them carefully so that they won't slip into the pond. Place an extra layer of liner or heavy landscaping fabric underneath them to cushion the stones and prevent them from wearing or gouging the liner material.

It's usually best to set the stones in 2 to 3 inches of mortar reinforced with chicken wire or metal lath. You can buy mortar premixed or make your own with a mix of 1 part cement and 3 parts sand. Any untreated mortar that comes in contact with the water, however, will make the water too alkaline and endanger the health of fish and plants. To remedy this, allow the mortar to cure for about a week. Then scrub the edging with a strong vinegar solution of 4 parts vinegar to 1 part water or a mix of 1 part muriatic (hydrochloric) acid to 2 parts tap water to neutralize the lime leaching from the mortar. You will then need to drain the pond, rinse the liner, and refill the pond with fresh water, repeating the process until the water tests neutral.

7 Add Plants Around the Perimeter. Tuck plants between rocks—either directly into the soil or in pots sunk into the ground—to soften the edges of the pond.

Planting-Shelf Options

Although some pond designs have shelves all the way around the perimeter for containerized plants, these are optional. On a practical level, you will often discover that containers are too big or the wrong shape for such shelves. Many water gardeners find that raising their containerized plants on bricks or plastic milk crates allows them to be more flexible about the placement of their marginal (shallow-water) plants. Another option is to create permanent planting areas that allow you to grow your plants without containers but still keep them from spreading.

To create planting areas for marginals, excavate a ledge wide enough for you to lay a stone or brick retaining wall along the outside edge on top of the liner. Mortar the stones just enough to keep them in place. (It's no problem to have water seeping between them.) Fill the area with garden soil. After planting, top the soil with gravel to keep it from dislodging. The shelf should be no wider than about a foot, so you can easily reach plants for maintenance.

Planting Pockets. Spaces between pondside stones allow for container plants or in-ground plantings. Give the latter good garden loam topped with gravel.

Planting Shelves. You can build permanent shelves into the side of your pond. But many water gardeners find that raising container plants on bricks, plastic crates, or other platforms gives them more flexibility in plant placement.

Planting Beds. In formal pools, some people use bricks to create permanent planters for water lilies in the middle of the pond. In a deep koi pond, permanent planting beds with edges 12 inches below the surface and 24 inches across will hold the largest water lilies and protect them from the fish. (Koi are less likely to bother plants this close to the surface.) For marginal plants, build the planter walls so that the edges are 6 inches below the surface to accommodate a wide range of species.

You can create deeper areas within the planter for species that need to grow 8 to 12 inches below the surface. Different plants grouped together look more natural in such beds, but obviously you can't rearrange them as easily as with containers. Such large planter beds are heavy; installing a concrete footing under your liner will help protect it.

Islands. Large ponds allow you to create islands for plants. These mounds can be slightly below water level for wetland or marginal plants, or above it for typical perennials or shrubs that need good drainage.

To create a wet island, shape a flat-topped mound of earth lower than the expected water level and cover it with the liner; build a retaining wall of upside-down sod pieces around the island perimeter, and fill the center area with heavy garden soil. For a dry island, build a flat-topped mound 6 to 12 inches higher than the expected water level and drape the liner over it. Cut a hole in the center of the liner. Dig organic matter into the soil before planting it with perennials or small shrubs. A layer of upside down sod can be used to hide the liner around the edges.

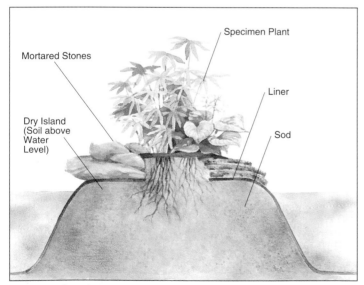

Plant Island. You can create either wet or dry islands, or both, to suit the types of plants you will be using. The wet island is just below the surface of the water with a retaining wall of sod; the dry island, above, is above the water level.

Extra Support for Pond Foundations

In sandy or crumbly soil, or where you'll be using large boulders for edging, it's a good idea to create additional support for the pond edges. The easiest way to do this is

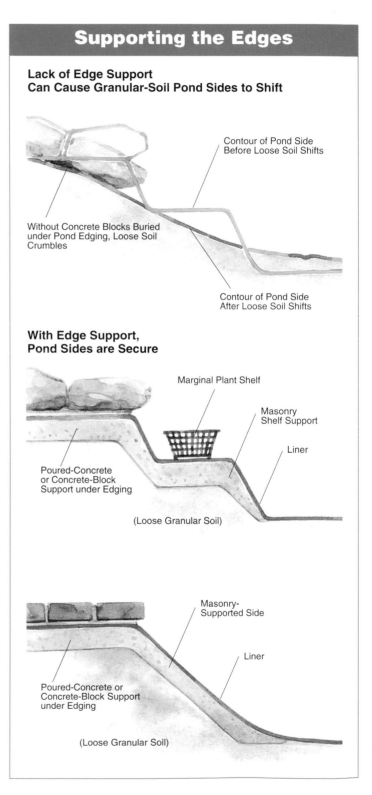

Supporting the Edges

Lack of Edge Support Can Cause Granular-Soil Pond Sides to Shift

Contour of Pond Side Before Loose Soil Shifts

Without Concrete Blocks Buried under Pond Edging, Loose Soil Crumbles

Contour of Pond Side After Loose Soil Shifts

With Edge Support, Pond Sides are Secure

Marginal Plant Shelf

Masonry Shelf Support

Liner

Poured-Concrete or Concrete-Block Support under Edging

(Loose Granular Soil)

Masonry-Supported Side

Liner

Poured-Concrete or Concrete-Block Support under Edging

(Loose Granular Soil)

by burying a line of concrete blocks along the edge of your pond site before excavating the pond. The blocks don't need to be touching, so it's possible to align them around an irregularly shaped pond. Buried blocks will also lend important additional support for plastic or fiberglass preformed pond shells; they'll help contain the substantial outward pressure exerted by water when a lined or preformed pond is filled. It will also be easier to lay stone edging without mortar on the resulting flat, solid surface. Use a spirit level to verify that all the blocks you install are level.

Bring the edge of your liner up and over the edges of the concrete blocks (or poured concrete). The installation of underlayment or heavy landscape fabric under the liner helps prevent punctures from the sharp edges of the blocks. The liner should extend at least a foot past the blocks, so the block material can be hidden. If you prefer to use poured concrete rather than blocks to strengthen the construction, bring in professional expertise. The foundation is far too important to cut corners.

Optional Concrete Overliner

A thin layer of concrete-like material spread over the liner will protect it from the damaging effects of ultraviolet rays as well as from punctures caused by waders in the pond. Plastic cement is the material of choice for a liner mixture because it contains latex additives that make the mixture highly resistant to cracking. Most lumberyards and masonry suppliers carry this product; mix 1 part plastic cement to 4 parts sand to make a good liner mixture. If you like, you can add coloring agents to the mixture and/or create various surface textures by brooming or troweling before it dries.

After installing the flexible liner, cover it with a layer of chicken wire to provide reinforcement. Hand-pack a 1-inch layer of plastic cement mixture into the chicken wire over the entire surface of the pond; wear heavy gloves for this procedure. Start packing mixture at the base of each sidewall, building up to the top in 6-foot-long sections. After the sidewalls are covered, do the pond bottom. Brush or trowel the surface smooth; then allow the plastic cement mixture to harden (about 10 to 12 hours, or overnight).

Once the material has hardened, fill the pond with water. Add 1 gallon of distilled white vinegar per 100 gallons of water; allow this mixture to stand one week. (The vinegar serves to neutralize the lime leaching from the cement.) Drain the pond. Rinse the

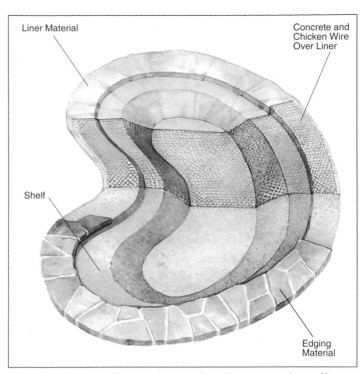

Liner Material

Concrete and Chicken Wire Over Liner

Shelf

Edging Material

Pond Supports. Sloping the pond walls may not be sufficient to stabilize them if the soil is very sandy or crumbly. Mortar may be needed to significantly strengthen the sides; a concrete overliner with chicken wire adds stability to the entire pond area. Apply to the pond sides and entire bottom.

overliner thoroughly before refilling the pond with fresh water. Test the pH of the water before adding fish or plants.

If the water tests too alkaline, it will be necessary to repeat the vinegar treatment and test again to ensure that the water has neutralized.

Edge Support. Provide support for the pond edge by installing a layer of concrete and reinforcing wire before adding the edge treatment.

Installing a Preformed Shell

Rigid, preformed pond shells of molded plastic or fiberglass are quick to install and resist punctures better than flexible liners. You don't have to fret about creating the design, and if you move out of your home, you could conceivably take the pond with you.

Preparing the Ground

Although the conditions for a rigid shell aren't as exacting as for a liner, the ground where you install a preformed pond must be free of rocks, projecting roots, and other sharp objects and—above all—must be stable. The shell, which can weigh several tons when full of water, will need to be fully supported by firm, well-packed earth. Any air pockets or bumps can cause it to crack or buckle.

Groundwater (from a high water table) can erode loose or sandy soil around the shell. In cold climates, frost heaving can deform or buckle it. If you anticipate either of these conditions, make the excavation about 6 to 8 inches deeper and wider than the shell. Then backfill the hole with 3 to 4 inches of smooth pea gravel, top with 2 inches of sand or finely sifted soil, and tamp firmly.

Preformed Shells. These durable plastic or fiberglass foundations come in many shapes and sizes, but won't allow you the unlimited design options of flexible liners.

Constructing a Preformed In-Ground Pool

1 Mark the Shell Outline. Except for very small ponds, you will need help with installation because you will be lifting and moving the shell several times. Place the preformed shell upright in the desired location. Use a plumb bob or a spirit level and stakes to transfer the shape of the pond rim to the ground, and mark the outline with a rope, garden hose, or nontoxic spray paint. Use stakes (spaced about 12 inches apart) to keep the rope or hose in place.

2 Dig and Prepare the Hole. Excavate the hole to conform to the shape of the pond shell, allowing an extra 2 inches around the pond perimeter and 2 inches in the bottom of the hole to be backfilled with sand to cushion the shell. If the shell has shallow-water shelves, dig the hole only to the depth of these shelves, and tamp the outside edges of the bottom firmly. Then put the shell in the hole, and mark the outline of the bottom of the pond. Remove the shell, and dig out this lower portion to the distance between the bottom of the shelves and the bottom of the pond (plus 2 extra inches). Flatten the bottom of the hole with the edge of a board, and firmly tamp the soil to provide a stable base for the shell. (Thinner shells in particular must have firm support under the shelves as well as on the sides and bottom.)

Remove any rocks or other sharp objects; then line the bottom of the hole with 2 to 3 inches of damp sand or finely sifted soil. Tamp all surfaces again. Use a spirit level to make sure the bottom of the excavation is perfectly level in all directions.

3 Set the Shell. Place the pond shell into the excavation, and check the height of the rim. The rim should be about 1 inch above the surrounding ground to prevent runoff from entering the pond. Add or remove sand from the bottom of the hole (and soil from the shelf support) until you achieve the desired height.

4 Level the Shell. Place a long, straight 2x4 across the shell rim in several places, and check with a spirit level. If the shell isn't level, pull it out of the hole and relevel the excavation. The pond must be perfectly level before you add any water. Even a few inches of water in the pond bottom will make the shell virtually impossible to move.

Backfill around the pond. Once the shell is level, start filling it with water slowly. As the water level rises, backfill the hole around the shell with sifted dirt or damp sand, tamping it gently with a shovel handle or the end of a 2x4. Make sure you fill any gaps or holes, especially around any shallow-water shelves. Check the rim for level frequently. Don't allow the water level inside the pond to rise above the backfilled earth outside the rim, or else the shell will tend to bulge outward. In other words, try to maintain equal pressure on both sides of the shell as you backfill.

5 Add Edging. When the shell is filled with water, you can conceal the exposed rim with rocks, masonry materials, or overhanging plants. If you use flagstones or flat pavers, allow them to overhang the pond edges by 1 to 2 inches. Don't allow the full weight of large rocks to rest on the pond rim, because the weight may deform or damage the pond walls. Instead, embed the rocks in a 3- to 4-inch-thick bed of mortar, raised slightly above the lip of the shell, or bury a line of concrete blocks along the rim of the shell. If you use mortar, neutralize the lime in it with distilled vinegar after the mortar has cured, as described in step 6 under "Constructing a Lined In-Ground Pond," (page 32).

Tools & Materials

- Preformed shell
- Plumb bob or spirit level and stakes
- Rope, garden hose, or nontoxic spray paint (for marking outlines)
- Shovel and tamper
- Damp sand or finely sifted soil
- Measuring tape ■ Long, straight 2x4
- Spirit level ■ Edging material
- Mortar and mixing equipment, vinegar, muriatic acid, or commercial concrete-curing agent (optional)

1 Use a plumb bob to mark the outline of the pre-formed shell on the ground.

2 Dig a hole that is 2 in. larger than the perimeter of the pond and 2 in. deeper than the shell.

3 Set the pond shell in the hole. The rim of the pond should be about 1 in. higher than grade.

4 Level the shell. Backfill around the shell using sand as you add water. Check the rim for level frequently.

5 Add edging, but don't allow the full weight of large rocks to rest on the rim of the shell.

chapter 4
streams & waterfalls

ALTHOUGH STILL PONDS HAVE THEIR OWN QUIET CHARM and create the most exquisite reflections, most people want to add movement and sound to their ponds through waterfalls, streams, fountains, or some combination of these. Such features also aerate the water, providing oxygen for fish and other pond life.

Design Pointers

The moving features you might add to your pond depend on its overall style as well as your terrain. If you have an informal pond, design your streams and falls to emulate those found in nature, and edge them with local rocks ranging in size from large boulders to small stones and pebbles. A crashing waterfall will look right on a steep natural slope. If you live in the flatlands, though, a waterfall more than 2 to 3 feet high will look artificial; consider a meandering stream instead. If you have a formal pool, possibilities include a straight-sided canal or water "stairs" that incorporate landscaping ties, poured-concrete slabs, precast concrete basins, masonry blocks or bricks, or even ceramic tiles.

In both formal pools and informal ponds, waterfalls and streams usually consist of a series of small pools or catch basins linked by low cascades. If space is limited, you can install a single raised basin above your pond, connected by one fall, or have a fall gush springlike from a fissure in a rock wall or ledge above the pond.

Building a successful watercourse is largely a matter of trial and error. To create the effect you want, you'll need to experiment with different sizes and shapes of rocks, as well as their placement in and around the watercourse. Before starting, give a good deal of thought to exactly the effect you want to create. Look at photographs of creeks and waterfalls. Take hikes along local streams, noting the size, shape, and texture of the rocks, and how the water moves over and around them. Study artificial streams and waterfalls in public gardens, in friends' gardens, and anywhere you can find them. Once you've gained access to these gardens, be sure to ask their owners about the hardware they used to get their effect, particularly the type and size of pump they installed. Just as genius is a mix of inspiration and perspiration, creating a successful watercourse is a mix of art and engineering.

Waterfalls

Keep a waterfall in scale with the pond. A small trickle in a large pond won't be very dramatic, nor will it be very effective at recirculating and oxygenating the water. And a large cascade gushing into a small pond will stir too much of the water surface, churning up sediment and making it nearly impossible to raise fish, water lilies, and other aquatic plants that prefer still water. If you want both a large, splashing fall and aquatic plants, you'll need to design the pond so plants can be placed well away from the wave action.

The smooth, flat flagstones used at the lip of this waterfall shape the flowing water into a wide, thin curtain.

Minimize Evaporation. To maintain the main pond's water level, the surface of the fall or stream should be smaller than that of the pond; a big, splashy water show can speed the loss of pond volume through evaporation. You can hold evaporation to a minimum by keeping the falls low and the watercourse relatively short. For the same reason, small, deep basins are preferable to large, shallow ones. As you proceed in the design and construction of your watercourse, you must also minimize any possibility of leaks between rocks along the bank and behind the falls.

Sight and Sound. Watercourses look best and are less prone to water loss when large, overhanging rocks are used for the lip of the falls. Use smooth, flat flagstones to produce a wide, thin curtain of water, or direct the water through a narrow gap between large boulders to produce a gushing effect. Creating a hollow space behind the falls will amplify and echo the sound of falling water. While the lips of informal falls are formed from naturalistic materials with irregular shapes, those of formal waterfalls can be brick, tile, flagstone, or landscaping ties. Some formal designs incorporate a sheet of clear acrylic plastic to create a wide, nearly transparent curtain of water. The plastic itself is all but invisible when the falls are in operation.

Shaping a Stream

For some people, a trickling rivulet is more picturesque than ocean waves. A winding stream is a particularly apt addition to a woodland or a rocky hillside; it's also at home on a prairie, where a waterfall would look contrived. Although you'll need a pond to feed your stream (unless you bury a water tank to take its place), you can make the stream the predominant feature by virtue of its length, placement, or elaborate planting and rock surrounds.

Stream Design. Nature usually arranges streams into a series of short, fairly flat sections separated by low falls or cascades. In a home water garden, streams need to be as level as possible so they will retain some water when the pump is turned off. Alternating between wet and dry conditions can shorten the life of plastic or fiberglass foundation materials, and crack mortar or concrete. A stream that holds some water at all times also looks more realistic. A drop of 1 to 2 inches per 10 feet is all that's needed to make the stream flow downhill. At that point, changes in width can change stream speed.

Stream Speed. To increase the speed of a stream's current, bring its banks closer together; for a more leisurely current, move the banks farther apart. If you want to grow shallow-water plants along the edges, a deep, wide, slow-moving stream will be preferable to a fast, narrow one. But avoid large areas of slow-moving shallow water, which can become clogged with thick mats of algae.

In either case, twists and turns in the course will make it look more realistic than will a straight channel. Vary the size of the rocks along the banks and the distance between the banks. Placing large rocks inside the watercourse will create rapids; placing smaller stones and pebbles will produce a rippling effect. Either approach will also make the stream look and sound more natural. Straight or parallel channels are appropriate only for formal designs.

Unlike most streams created by Mother Nature, this watercourse was designed to be fairly level to maintain a minimum amount of water at all times.

Choosing and Buying a Liner

To prevent water loss between rocks or other edging, artificial waterfalls and streams are lined with the same types of materials that are used to line a pond. Most of the same purchasing, design, and installation considerations also apply. In addition to the liner, remember to purchase sufficient underlayment material to cover the entire watercourse.

Flexible Liners

The easiest and most versatile material to use is a flexible liner, which will adapt to both formal and informal waterfall designs. Ideally, you should use one large piece of liner for constructing both the main pond and the waterfall or stream to provide a continuous, seamless barrier. In practice, though, it's not always easy to align one large square or rectangular sheet of liner with the selected watercourse site without creating large amounts of waste material.

How Much Liner? To determine the amount of liner you'll need for your watercourse, measure the width and length of the course, and then add twice the depth of the fall or stream plus 2 feet to allow a foot of overlap on each side. If you plan to create wetland areas to either side of your fall or stream, add in this additional width. If you'll be piecing the liner along its length, add at least 12 inches (for each junction) to allow sufficient overlap to prevent leakage at joints. When planning the main pond, make sure the liner for the main pond is large enough to extend upward into the first catch basin.

Using a Flexible Liner

Flexible Liner Watercourse. The same material used for the pond bottom is used for the waterfall or stream.

Stone to Hold Liner

Hose

Excavation for Plants

Liner Material

Catch Basin

Liner Joint Overlap

Edging Stones

Plantings

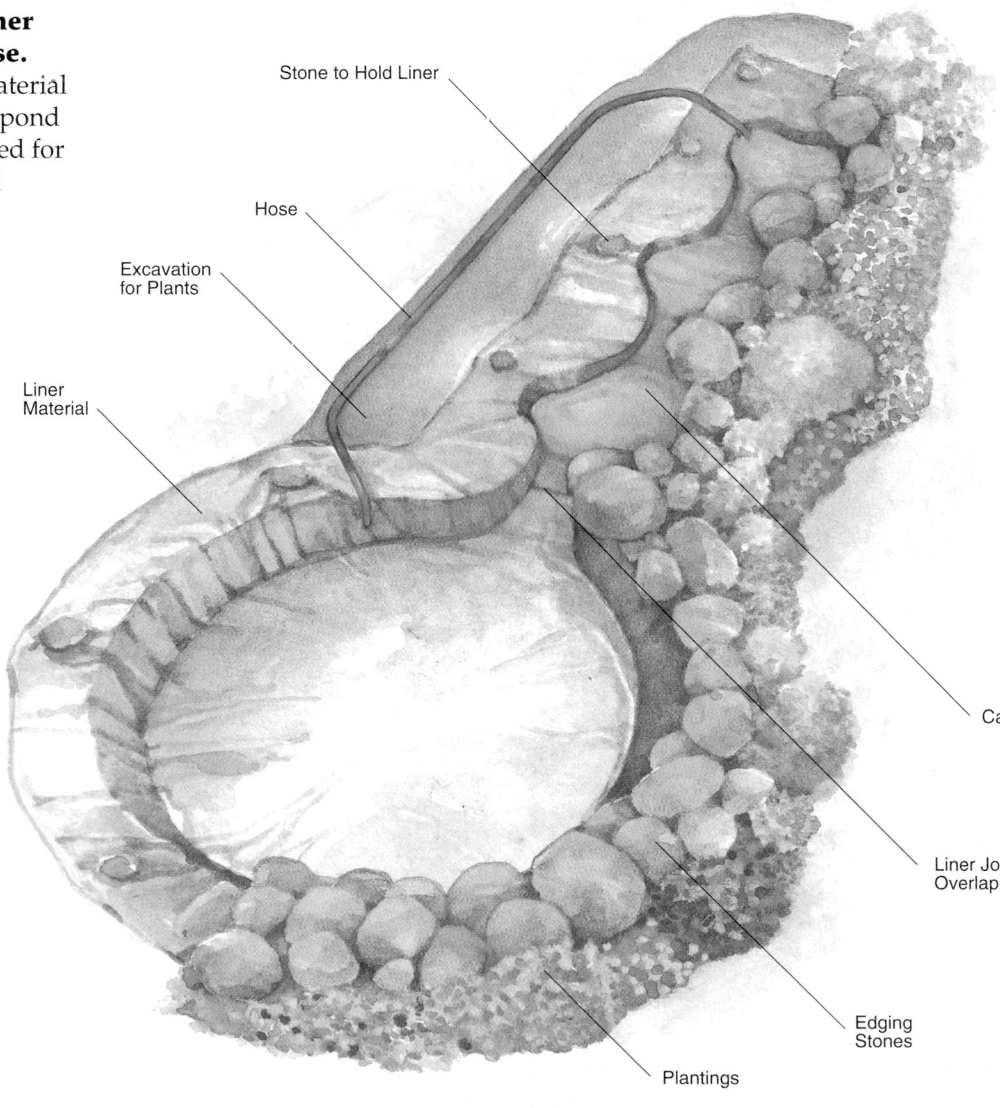

Preformed Waterfalls

Most companies that make preformed fiberglass or plastic ponds also offer preformed waterfall runs or courses of the same material. The units come in many different sizes and colors, although black is among the most popular. Preformed waterfalls are installed much like a preformed rigid pond shell. (See "Installing a Preformed Shell" in Chapter 3, page 36.) The units consist of one or more small basins with built-in cascades and a lower lip that empties into the pond. You can combine two or more short watercourses to produce a longer watercourse, with each unit emptying into the one below it.

Styles. Informal preformed watercourses are shaped (and sometimes colored) to simulate natural rock, although most will look artificial unless the edges are disguised with overhanging stones or other materials. Formal preformed waterfalls are usually smaller versions of square or rectangular preformed ponds, with the addition of a built-in lip or spillway.

Materials. Fiberglass and plastic watercourses are lightweight and inexpensive. But as with preformed ponds, the sizes and designs are limited. In fact, preformed watercourses are often designed for use with a specific pump size. On the other hand, you may find it an advantage that your design has been worked out in advance, since you can skip some planning and measuring. Preformed watercourses made of cement or reconstituted stone are also available. Although these are more substantial and natural-looking than plastic or fiberglass units, they are much heavier. As a result, the practical size of these units is limited to only a few square feet.

Choosing a Pump for Moving Water

The water for your fall, stream, or fountain is recirculated from your pond by a small electric pump. Water-garden suppliers sell a wide variety of pumps made specifically for ponds. Your first step is to choose a pump big enough to operate your waterfall and any other water feature in your pond.

Sizing the Pump

In general for a waterfall, a pump that recirculates one-half of the pond's total water volume per hour will provide the minimum flow required to produce a pleasing proportion of moving water for the size of the pond. For example, if the pond holds 1,000 gallons of water, you should select a pump that will deliver at least 500 gallons per hour at the top of the falls. For a larger, bolder cascade, select a pump that will turn over the full 1,000 gallons in one hour. It's better to err on the side of a too-large pump than have one that's too small.

Another way to determine pump size is to calculate the amount of water required for cascades of various sizes. First, measure the width of the spillway over which the water will flow. Then decide how deep you want the water where it flows over the lip. For a light sheet of water (¼ inch deep), you'll need a pump that produces 50 gallons per hour for each inch of lip width. For a heavy flow (1 inch deep), look for a pump that produces 150 gallons per hour for each inch of lip width. For example, if the falls will be 6 inches wide, you'll need a pump that can deliver 300 gallons per hour for a ¼-inch-deep flow, or one that delivers 900 gallons per hour for a 1-inch-deep flow.

Determining Pond Capacity

In order to buy the right size pump, you need to figure your pond's capacity in gallons of water. (You'll also need this information for choosing a filter and determining correct dosages of plant fertilizers, fish medications, algaecides, and other chemical treatments.)

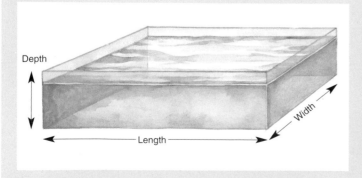

The most accurate way to determine pond capacity is to attach a flow meter to your faucet or water-supply line and record the number of gallons used when you fill the pond.

Here's a less accurate but easier and less expensive method: turn on the garden hose at a steady flow rate, and time how long it takes to fill a 5-gallon bucket (say, 10 seconds). Then time how many minutes it takes to fill the pond at the same flow rate (say, 20 minutes). Now figure out the flow rate of the hose in gallons per minute (5 gallons in 10 seconds x 6 = 30 gallons per minute). Next, multiply the gallons per minute by the number of minutes it took to fill the pond (30 gallons x 20 minutes = 600 gallons). If it isn't practical to fill (or refill) the pond with water, calculate capacity in gallons using one of the following formulas. Each assumes that the pond sides are straight (or steeply sloped) and that the bottom is flat.

Pump Head (Lift). When shopping for a pump, check the performance charts that come with the product. Most pumps are rated in gallons per hour at various heights above the water surface. This height is referred to as head or lift. The higher you place the discharge for the waterfall above the pond, the lower the pump output (because the higher your waterfall, the harder the pump has to push to deliver water to the top). For example, a pump that delivers 300 gallons at a 1-foot head may deliver only 120 gallons at a 4-foot head.

In pump-performance charts, manufacturers also provide a maximum head figure, which is the theoretical maximum height to which the pump can lift water. For best pump performance, purchase a pump whose maximum head height is well above the total height of the falls. You can buy moderately priced pumps offering a maximum head height of more than 20 feet.

If you intend to incorporate a fountain in addition to your waterfall, you need to add to your overall figure the gallons per hour required to operate the fountain. If you're adding fish, you'll need a separate mechanical or biological filter, which will further restrict flow and thus necessitate a bigger pump. (Your choice of filters will be limited with certain types of pumps; other pumps are more versatile. See "Filtration" on page 73 for more on filters.)

Pump Performance

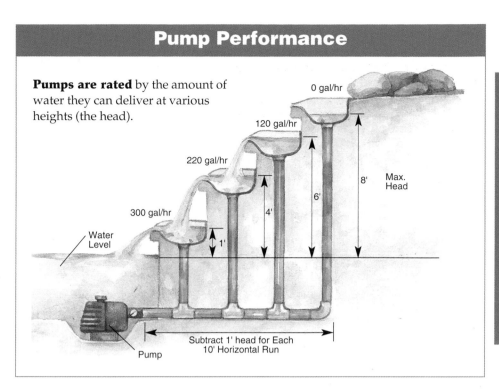

Pumps are rated by the amount of water they can deliver at various heights (the head).

0 gal/hr

120 gal/hr

220 gal/hr

300 gal/hr

Water Level

8' Max. Head

6'

4'

1'

Pump

Subtract 1' head for Each 10' Horizontal Run

- **Rectilinear ponds:** If the pond is roughly square or rectangular, measure its average depth, width, and length. Then multiply the three figures to determine cubic feet. Multiply the cubic feet by 7.5 to get capacity in gallons.

- **Circular ponds:** Multiply one-half the diameter by one-half the diameter (which equals radius squared) by 3.14 by the depth by 7.5 for gallon volume.

- **Oval ponds:** Multiply one-half the width by one-half the length by 3.14 by the depth by 7.5 for gallon volume.

- **Free-form ponds:** It's tough to accurately calculate an irregularly shaped pond's volume. For the closest estimate, determine the average depth, width, and length, and then use the equation for oval ponds.

Other Considerations. Placing the recirculating pump or pump inlet close to the falls increases the pump's efficiency, because the pump then needs to push the water a shorter distance. (You'll also need less tubing or pipe between the pump and the head of the falls.) As a rule, every 10 feet of horizontal pipe or tubing is equal to 1 foot of vertical rise in reducing the performance of the pump. Thus, theoretically, you could power a 30-foot stream with the same pump you would need for a 3-foot waterfall. (That's only theoretical, since the stream will have a modest incline, and the fall will have at least a short horizontal run.)

Buy a pump slightly more powerful than you think you'll need. Some pumps have valves that let you adjust the flow. If yours doesn't, you can restrict the flow by installing a separate valve on the outlet, or discharge, side of the pump or by using a special restriction clamp that attaches to the outlet tubing. (Never restrict the flow on the outlet side by more than 25 percent, or you'll burn out the motor.) Before buying the pump, find out if the dealer will allow you to exchange it for a larger size if it turns out to be too small to operate the waterfall to your satisfaction.

Submersible or External? Submersible pumps are submerged in the water and removed only periodically to allow cleaning of the built-in filter or strainer that keeps out leaves and other debris. Submersible pumps are used in most garden ponds for a number of good reasons. They run cooler and more quietly than external pumps and are often less expensive. They are usually more economical to install and operate because they require less plumbing. Reasonably priced models range in capacity from 180 to 1,200 gallons per hour; high-capacity models will handle up to 3,400 gallons per hour.

Adjustable Flow Submersible Pump

1200 gph Submersible Pump with Prefilter

500 gph Submersible Pump

Pump Kit with Fountainhead

If a submersible pump doesn't work with your pond design, you can buy a pump designed to operate either in open air or submerged. Compact in size, these devices are a good compromise in situations where a submersible pump would pose safety hazards or be prone to damage, or where a typical external pump would be too big for the pond. Their capacities are similar to those of submersible pumps. For external operation, these pumps usually need to be placed in a dry sump below the water level of the pond. Dig a hole deep enough to accommodate the pump but above the water table; provide a cover for the hole that's easy to camouflage and to remove for inspection or maintenance.

External pumps are those that sit outside the water, like those used for swimming pools. They're usually appropriate only for very large waterfalls and fountains, or in situations where a submersible pump would be dangerous or impractical—such as in a pond that doubles as a wading pool. With capacities ranging from 2,400 to more than 8,000 gallons per hour and a maximum head of up to 80 feet, external pumps are overkill for most backyard ponds, and the noise they make can distract from the pleasant sounds of your water feature. They also require their own housing to protect them (which is difficult to camouflage). If you're installing a swimming pool, though, you might consider plumbing the pump and filtration system to operate a pond and waterfall also.

Determining Quality

When selecting a pump, buy the best you can afford—even if you're buying only a small one. The least expensive (and least durable) pumps have a relatively short life span. Suitable only for relatively small water features, they also tend to clog more easily.

Moderate-Quality Pumps. Most moderately priced pumps have aluminum or cast-iron housings with a corrosion-resistant epoxy finish. They tend to be tougher and more impact-resistant than plastic pumps and come in a wide range of capacities. Aluminum-housed pumps are the less expensive of these two types, and will corrode more quickly in salt water, chlorinated water, or water frequently treated with pond chemicals.

High-Quality Pumps. The most long-lasting—and expensive—pumps are a combination of brass, bronze, and stainless-steel components. These pumps will withstand a variety of water conditions—including salty and chlorinated water—and can operate continuously. As a rule, they come only in larger sizes (capacities of 800 gallons per hour or higher). If your pond will be a permanent feature in your yard, these pumps are worth the extra cost.

Efficiency. When selecting a pump, also consider energy efficiency. Compare the pump's amp rating (or wattage, if it's given) to its output in gallons per hour. If two pumps have the same output, the one with the lower amp rating is more energy efficient. And make sure the cord is long enough to reach your planned or existing electrical outlet. Many pumps come with a 6-foot cord, which won't work if local codes require the electrical outlet to be 6 or more feet away from the pond edge. You can usually order longer cords from the pump manufacturer as an option. Use only cords and plugs designed for use with the pump. Don't use extension cords unless they have a built-in ground-fault circuit interruptor (GFCI).

It's a good idea to order all the required fittings, valves, and pipe needed to operate your waterfall at the same time you order your pump, as well as other features, such as a separate filter or fountain.

Electrical Requirements

Your pond will require an underground electrical cable from your home's power source, not only for a pump but also for any underwater or perimeter lighting. In many municipalities, a licensed electrician must do the wiring. In all cases, to ensure safety and to avoid expensive reinstallation, check local codes for outdoor electrical requirements before you start.

Outdoor Components. Make sure all outlets, wiring, and connections are designed for outdoor use. The National Electric Code (NEC) does not require that you put the cable in conduit, but local codes may require this. When a circuit is protected by GFCI as that for any pond must be, the NEC requires only that the cable be 12 inches deep. But consider burying the cable at least 18 inches deep to prevent it from being disturbed by spades, rototillers, or other gardening equipment. Exterior electrical boxes, shielded cable, and PVC conduit are available at local hardware stores.

Pumps. Most small submersible pumps come with a waterproof cord that you simply plug into a three-prong electrical outlet near the pond site. You must protect this receptacle with GFCI in a weatherproof outlet box with a watertight-while-in-use lid. With some larger pumps (both submersible and external), you hardwire the cord directly into a circuit, enclosing the connection in a weatherproof junction box near the pond. The latter requires a GFCI breaker wired into the circuit, either in the main electrical panel or in a subpanel. In either case, you should wire a switch into the circuit so that you can control the pump and lights from inside the house. If possible, locate the outlet or junction box in an inconspicuous and protected area, such as under a deck or against the side of a building. Although you may be able to tap into an existing circuit in the house, it's best to put the pump and pond lights on a separate circuit, with their own breaker at the main service panel. If you tap into an existing branch circuit, make sure it has sufficient capacity to handle the additional load of the pump and any outdoor lighting you might choose to install later.

Plumbing Your Moving Water Feature

Plumbing for most pumps is relatively simple. Complexity will vary depending on the pump model, the length of the pipe between pump and outlet, and the number of water features the pump will operate.

Locate the pump as close as possible to your moving water feature. For submersible types, this usually means placing it at the base of the falls (or statue). Remember to raise submersible pumps a few inches off the pond bottom with a brick or a stone to prevent silt and other sediment from clogging the pump intake. For nonsubmersible types, you'll have to use your creativity to find a spot that's relatively close to the pond yet as unobtrusive as possible.

Eyesore? Bulky and noisy, external pumps are hard to hide in the landscape and are appropriate only for the largest waterfalls.

Tubing. Some pumps are sold with a length of inexpensive clear plastic tubing, which is a larger-diameter version of the type used for aquarium pumps. Although such tubing is adequate for short runs, it has several drawbacks. First, the thin walls of the tubing are easily crushed or kinked, so you can't bury it underground or make it conform to sharp bends. Conversely, if the tubing is exposed to sunlight, algae will build up on the inner walls, restricting flow. Because exposure to sunlight will eventually make the tubing brittle, it must be replaced periodically.

One solution is to run a short piece of flexible tubing from the pump to the edge of the pond, connecting it to a rigid PVC pipe that runs from there to the top catch basin at the head of the falls. Alternatively, you can use a higher-grade flexible tubing for the entire run, either a reinforced type or a special black-vinyl tubing sold by pump suppliers. Make sure the diameter of the tubing meets or exceeds the size recommended for your pump model, since a smaller diameter will restrict water flow.

Plumbing Waterfalls. When plumbing the waterfall, keep sharp bends and right-angle pipe junctions to a minimum, as these tend to restrict flow. Lay the outlet tube along the ground as close as possible to the edge of the watercourse. Camouflage the outlet tube where it runs between the pond and the top of the watercourse with rocks, plants, or mulch. It's best not to mortar it permanently behind your landscape rocks, because you'll need easy access to deal with any future maintenance problems.

Water Pressure. When you run the end of the outlet hose or pipe into the top of the watercourse, you may find that the water pressure produces a strong jet, causing water to splash outside the catch basin. If this happens, either run the hose under a small pile of rocks in the catch basin, or fit a short section of larger perforated pipe or hose over the end of the outlet to break the force.

Fittings

Pump suppliers offer a wide range of fittings and adapters to connect pumps to various water features. Use nontoxic plastic valves and fittings wherever possible; brass and other metal fittings can corrode with time and may be toxic to fish. Most fittings for flexible plastic tubing are a barbed, push-fit type; when using these fittings, install hose clamps at all connections to prevent leaks. Fittings and connections for rigid PVC pipe are either screwed on or welded on using PVC cement. Some pumps require brass fittings on the pump discharge, which may or may not include a flow-control valve. Depending on the pump design, you may need to install an adapter fitting so that you can attach flexible tubing or rigid PVC pipe.

If you add a tee-fitting with a diverter valve to your pump discharge as shown in the drawing below, you will be able to operate two water features, such as a fountain

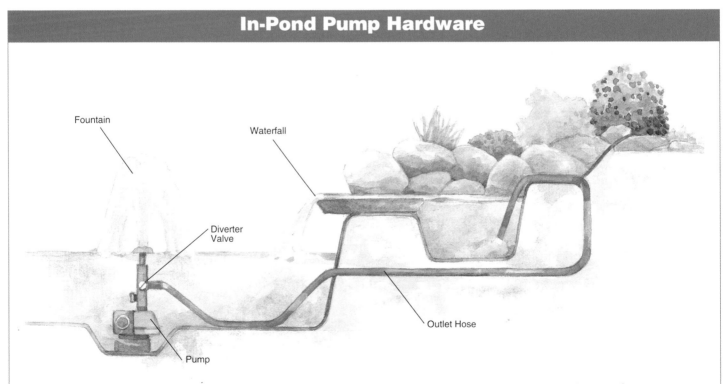

In-Pond Pump Hardware

Fountain

Waterfall

Diverter Valve

Pump

Outlet Hose

The right fittings and valves, in this case a tee-fitting and a diverter valve, let you run several water features simultaneously.

Maintain Pond Levels Automatically with a Float Valve

Ponds and fountains recirculate water, but even so, you'll need to top off the water level every so often. This is particularly true in small ponds during hot weather. Fortunately, you can eliminate this chore by installing a float valve. When the water level drops, this device lowers, automatically triggering a valve to open and allow more water to be fed into the pond through a pipe or tubing connected to a nearby faucet. You can find these inexpensive setups at nurseries that carry water-garden accessories or catalog and Internet suppliers.

Clamp the float valve to a short steel rod mortared between stones just below the waterline. Connect the valve to the main water supply with a ¼-inch diameter copper or plastic tube. Prevent pond water from siphoning back into the water supply by installing a back-flow preventor (also called an anti-siphon device). You can get one that screws onto the faucet—be careful to install it facing the right direction. Also install a check valve on the faucet before you install the backflow preventer.

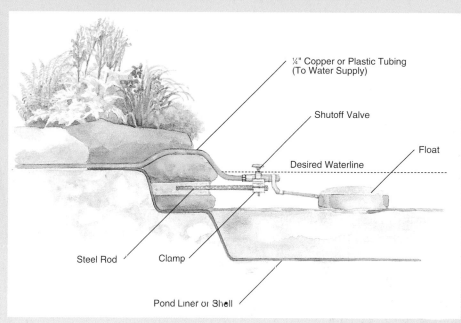

¼" Copper or Plastic Tubing (To Water Supply)

Shutoff Valve

Float

Desired Waterline

Steel Rod

Clamp

Pond Liner or Shell

and a waterfall, at the same time. However, you can accomplish the same result by installing a plain tee-fitting plus an in-line flow-control valve in the shorter of the two pipe runs. Both types of fittings will allow you to regulate the amount of water that is supplied to each feature. If you don't install a diverter or flow-control valve, the pumped water will take the path of least resistance (i.e., the shorter pipe run). The result will be either too little flow to operate one feature or too much flow to the other, or both. The pump should have enough capacity to operate all attached features.

Good Planning. As with all aspects of your pond design, careful planning is paramount. If you buy a pump with the intent of operating only one water feature and decide later that you would like to add more, you will face the choice of either buying a new, larger-capacity pump to run all the features simultaneously, or buying a second pump. The latter choice would allow you to power them independently (so that you can run your waterfall but not your fountain and vice versa), but may require additional electrical work or the use of an outlet that was originally planned for lighting. Water garden suppliers report that return customers inevitably want larger ponds with additional features. Thus your best bet may be to think big in the beginning and plan for all future contingencies.

A float valve hidden under the rock wall automatically maintains the pond's water level during dry spells.

Installing a Submersible Pump

Submersible pumps add movement and sound to a water garden. They're very easy to install and relatively uncomplicated to maintain. If the pump will be used only for filtration, place the submersible pump/filter in your sump or in the deepest part of the pond. Run the outlet tube to the far end of the pond for better circulation. If the pump will be feeding water to a waterfall or fountain, locate the pump as close as possible to the foot of the falls or the fountain. Plumbing connections at the outlet hose (or pipe) must be high quality, and all necessary electrical connections must meet your town's required electrical codes. Raise the pump several inches off the pond bottom to prevent frequent filter clogging.

Basic Installation Tips
- Place pump on a brick at the bottom of the pond.
- Keep bends and right angles in tubing to a minimum in order not to reduce flow.
- Disguise all hoses and electrical lines under mulch or rocks.

Tools & Materials
- Submersible Pump/Filter Kit
- Outlet hose and fittings (sufficient length from pump to top pool of falls)
- Electrical outlet accessibility
- Platform material (to raise pump off pond floor)
- Material (stone, gravel) to hide lines and cables

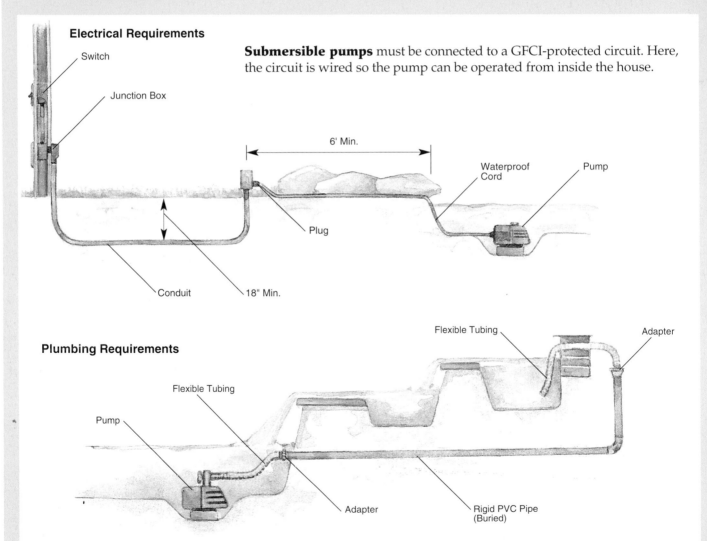

Electrical Requirements

Switch

Junction Box

6' Min.

Waterproof Cord

Pump

Plug

Conduit

18" Min.

Submersible pumps must be connected to a GFCI-protected circuit. Here, the circuit is wired so the pump can be operated from inside the house.

Plumbing Requirements

Flexible Tubing

Adapter

Flexible Tubing

Pump

Adapter

Rigid PVC Pipe (Buried)

For long pipe runs, bury rigid PVC pipe in a trench alongside the waterfall. Connect the pump to the pipe with a short length of flexible tubing. This enables you to easily remove the pump from the pond for cleaning and maintenance. Secure all connections using hose clamps.

Installing a Lined Watercourse

If you're using a flexible plastic or rubber liner for your pond, it's easiest to excavate for the watercourse and install its liner at the same time. You can, however, also add a lined watercourse to an existing pond with any material at a later time.

1 Grade the Site. If you're working on flat ground, you may want to rough out the shape **(A)** of your watercourse before you begin changing the grade. Then build up a berm of compacted soil next to the pond at your waterfall location (this is a good way to make use of the soil excavated from the pond). Make the berm wide enough to accommodate the watercourse, with sufficient space around the perimeter for rocks, plants, and other landscaping materials. Tamp the soil firmly to compact it. Slope the sides gently away from the proposed excavation to prevent rain from washing dirt into the watercourse. Avoid steeply sloped mounds, which not only look unnatural but will be more prone to soil erosion. If you are working on a naturally sloping site, especially one that is very rocky, it will dictate the shape of your watercourse to a great extent. Now working on your slope—natural or otherwise—cut a series of level terraces to create what looks like a staircase. Each terrace will serve as a catch basin for your waterfall or stream. For a stream, you will have long steps with short risers; for a steep waterfall, you will have shorter steps with taller risers. Make each step large enough to accommodate rocks or other edging material or concrete supporting blocks if you are using them **(B)**.

Tools & Materials

- Flour, nontoxic spray paint, or stakes and string (for marking outlines)
- Shovel
- Tamper for compacting soil (or a scrap of 2x6 nailed to the end of a long 2x4)
- Spirit level
- Long, straight 2x4 (for checking level of large areas)
- Concrete blocks (optional, to provide increased support for outer edges and/or waterfall lip)
- Pump, tubing, and connecting fixtures
- Adhesive or tape for liner joints (optional)
- Heavy-duty scissors or utility knife for cutting liner and underlayment
- Underlayment
- Liner
- 3-inch or longer nails (to hold liner in position)
- Edging material such as rocks
- Mortar (optional, for securing stones along edges)
- Landscaping materials (rocks, plants)
- Watering can or hose

1a Rough out the shape of your watercourse; then build up a berm of compacted soil next to your waterfall location. Tamp the soil firmly to compact it.

1b Cut a series of level steps to serve as catch basins; make each step large enough to accommodate supporting materials such as concrete blocks.

(continued on page 50)

(continued from page 49)

2 **Creating Catch Basins.** You want each one of your stair steps to hold water even when the pump is turned off. Things will always look natural as a result. There are several ways you can accomplish this. If you are using concrete block supports, which is essential when you are working with either sandy or flinty soil, they will form the sides of your catch basin. (They will look

straight and artificial, but you will make them look natural later by artful placement of rocks on top of and around them). Dig your terrace, and shape it so that it slopes backward slightly, away from the pond.

If you are working with clay soil that packs solidly, you may not need concrete blocks. Instead, you can excavate a catch basin in the middle of each stair, leaving a ledge of earth on which to place your edging stones. (Even if you have clay soil, however, the concrete blocks are a good idea if you are edging your stream with large, heavy boulders.)

If the basin is large enough, you may want to cut another ledge around the perimeter in which to set partially submerged boulders. But remember that the finished watercourse will look smaller than the excavated holes once the rocks or other edging materials are in place along the sides.

The catch basins are miniature versions of the main pond, so be sure to follow the procedures outlined in steps 1 through 7 on pages 30–33 to dig and level the basins. As with your pond, your stream should be level across its width. To make sure that it is, use a spirit level placed on top of a 2x4.

Now you need to provide a stable base for the waterfall lip of your terrace or catch basin on the leading edge, which is the edge that is the closest to the pond. You can do this by creating a berm that is at least 12 inches wide. You can use well-compacted soil, but again, when you are dealing with loose or sandy soil, it is a good idea to use concrete blocks or poured concrete to create a more solid base.

2 Dig your terraces and shape them so that they slope backward slightly, away from the pond.

3a Run the pipe from the point where it exits the pond to the top catch basin or head of the falls.

3b Make sure all fittings go together securely so that no leaks occur.

3 Install the Tubing and Pump. Position your pump at the foot of the lowest falls. (Elevate it on a brick or a flat stone; raising it a few inches off the bottom will keep sediment from clogging the pump intake.) If your pump isn't a submersible type, put it close to the base of the falls. Run the pipe or tubing **(A)** from the pump alongside the watercourse from the point where it exits the pond to the top catch basin or head of the falls. (For more information on choosing and installing pumps, see pages 42-48.) All fittings must go together securely so no leaks occur **(B).**

4 Position the Liners. If you're using underlayment, position it first **(A).** If you're using a single liner for the pond and watercourse, drape the liner over the entire excavation and over the supporting concrete blocks if you have used them **(B).** Then slowly fill the pond with water to hold the liner in place, allowing the liner to settle before filling the watercourse.

If you're using separate pieces of liner, start by fitting the liner for the main pond, allowing enough overlap at the waterfall end to extend up and over the first waterfall lip. Cut and fit the next piece of liner in the lowest catch basin, providing at least 12 inches of overlap with the main-pond liner. Overlap the liners for additional catch basins in the same manner.

For additional protection against leaks, you can join adjacent liner sections with a special liner adhesive or tape, although with sufficient overlap this is not necessary.

Next, it's important to check for level. Use a watering can or hose to fill the catch basin(s) with water to settle the liner in place, as you did for the pond.

Check for leaks, and note the water level around the rim of each basin. If you see any high or low spots, remove or add soil beneath the liner to level the basin.

Then, to keep the liner in place while you add edging material around the water feature, push large nails through the liner into the ground every foot or so around the overlapping edges. (Note: you do not have to remove the nails later.)

You can also use large stones to keep the liner positioned until you have installed your edging.

4a Drape the underlayment over the entire excavation and over the supporting concrete blocks if you have used them.

4b Install the liner, fitting it into position as necessary. Be sure to cover the concrete blocks if using.

(continued on page 52)

(continued from page 51)

5a Position overhanging rocks or other edging materials across and on either side of the waterfall lip.

5b Make sure the top surface of the lip stones are just slightly below the water level of the stream or basin above.

5c The shape, size, and position of the last stone laid will determine the pattern of the waterfall as it enters the pond.

5 Position the Edging Stones. Start by positioning the overhanging rocks or other edging materials **(A)** across the waterfall lip **(B)** and on either side of it. For a more natural effect, you can also place stones behind the waterfall, beneath the lip, to hide the liner. The top surface of the lip stones should be just slightly below the water level of the stream or basin above, so that water will flow from one basin to the next without overflowing the banks. The last major stone to be laid is the one on the exit spillway **(C)**. The characteristics of this stone and its positioning will determine the pattern of the waterfall entering the pond.

6 Fine-tune the Waterfall. Now install your pump. (See "Installing a Submersible Pump" on page 48.) Turn on the pump and notice how water flows over the lip; adjust the height and angle of the stones, if necessary, to provide a pleasing cascade. When you're satisfied with the results, place your remaining stones along the edge of each basin on top of your concrete blocks, along the ledge you've shaped around the perimeter of each basin, or along the stream banks. Hide the liner edges with the edging rocks or bury it with soil. Mortaring the rocks will prevent them from slipping into the watercourse. You can arrange stones in the watercourse to alter the flow pattern, but avoid using gravel because it will become clogged with algae and silt.

Last, add landscaping. For a natural look, arrange additional rocks on and around the mound for the waterfall and near the stream. Use boulders, medium-size rocks, and pebbles to avoid making the waterfall area look like a pile of rocks. Make planting pockets between stones for low shrubs, grasses, ground covers, and other plants.

6 After installing your pump, turn it on to check how the water flows over the lip; if necessary, adjust the height and angle of the stones to create a pleasing cascade. Place remaining stones.

Installing a Preformed Watercourse

Just as with a lined watercourse, you can install a preformed watercourse at the same time as your pond or add it later. If you're installing more than one unit, see the instructions in step 5 before beginning.

1 Grade the Site. If you're working with a natural slope above the pond, excavate a pocket in which to place the watercourse. On flat ground, build up a berm of firm soil to support the shell at the appropriate height above the pond (you can use the soil from the pond excavation). The sides of the berm should slope gently away from the watercourse and be wide enough to accommodate the rocks or other landscape materials used to disguise the edges of the watercourse. Firmly tamp the built-up soil to provide support for the unit. Test the firmness of the soil to see that the watercourse won't sink unevenly into it. Next, set the preformed watercourse in position on top of the mound and mark its outline on the ground with flour, nontoxic spray paint, or a series of short stakes.

2 Dig the Hole. Now dig a hole within the outline you made to match the size and shape of your preformed watercourse unit. It's important to tamp the soil down firmly; if fiberglass and plastic units lack firm support on the sides and bottom, they will bend and warp when filled with water. If your soil is loose or sandy, you may need to create extra support for the sides of your pond with an encircling collar of concrete blocks. This will also provide additional support for rocks or other edging materials. (See "Extra Support for Pond Foundations," on page 34.) Lay the unit in place to see if it fits. If not, lift it out and either add or remove soil as necessary to conform to the shape of the shell. (continued on page 54)

Tools & Materials

- Preformed watercourse
- Pump, tubing, and connecting fixtures
- Flour, nontoxic spray paint, or stakes
- Landscaping materials (rocks, plants)
- Concrete blocks (optional)
- Mortar (optional)
- Shovel, fine sand, ruler (to measure sand depth)
- Tamper for compacting soil
- Cement and mixing equipment (only for precast stone and cement units)
- Spirit level and long, straight 2x4

1 Build up a soil berm and set the unit in position. Mark the outline of a watercourse on the ground.

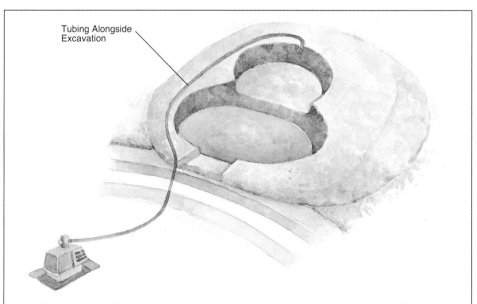

Tubing Alongside Excavation

2 Excavate a hole to recess the unit into the side of the berm, or hill, above the pond. Run the pump outlet hose to the head of the watercourse.

(continued from page 53)

3 Place the Watercourse. Position the watercourse in the excavation so that its lip or spillway overlaps the pond edge. Use a spirit level to make sure the basin or basins of the watercourse are level in all directions. Check from about a half dozen positions on each basin to be sure your shell is level and should not shift positions. (If your spirit level isn't long enough, place a straight 2x4 across the rim and put the level on the 2x4.) Backfill around the edges with fine sand, packing it firmly into the excavation and checking for level frequently. Remember to backfill the space between concrete blocks if you have used them. Build the backfilled sand to a height of 1 to 2 inches below the outside edge of the shell (flange), or as recommended by the manufacturer.

Now run the length of pipe outlet tubing alongside the watercourse and into the top basin. Secure the tubing in place at the top of the watercourse with rocks, or as specified in the manufacturer's instructions, in preparation for testing it.

4 Test the Watercourse. Fill the unit with water and check the water level around the rim to make sure the unit remained level during the backfilling. If you haven't already done so, install the pump, attach the outlet tubing to it, and fill the main pond. Then pump water down the course. The water should flow evenly over the lip and any built-in cascades at a level of about 1 inch below the rim. Adjust the pump flow rate if necessary.

5 Place any Additional Units. If you'll be installing additional sections of watercourse, follow steps 1 through 3 to install each successive unit of watercourse above the first. After installing and leveling each one, you'll need to test it by filling it with water and allowing the water to run down the rest of the course (step 4). Make any needed adjustments at this time to the height and position of the unit. Make sure each unit is firmly positioned before installing the one above.

Turn on the pond pump. When all of the units are in place, position the pump outlet pipe or tubing at the top of the watercourse. Some units have built-in pipe or hose fittings for this purpose. With others, you can attach a short piece of plastic tubing to the outlet pipe; run the tubing over the rim at the top of the watercourse, and disguise the tubing with rocks or plants. Run the watercourse continuously for 48 hours, then recheck it for any settling and readjust the flow or the position of the hose if necessary.

6 Add Landscaping. Depending on the design of the unit, you may be able to use rocks or overhanging plants to disguise the edges of the watercourse and help

3 Place the watercourse in the excavation, and check that it is level. Backfill to hold the unit in place.

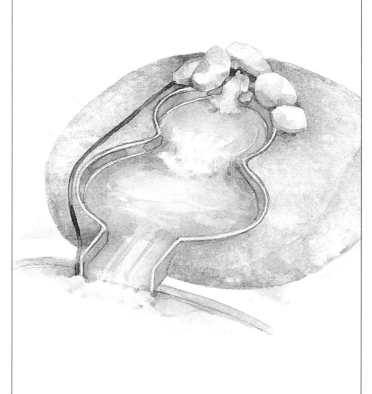

4 Turn on the pump and run water down the unit to make sure it works properly.

blend it into the surrounding landscape. If you're setting large rocks or boulders around the rim, be careful that their weight doesn't crush or buckle the shell. A collar of concrete blocks buried around the edge of your watercourse will provide additional support. (See "Extra Support for Pond Foundations," on page 34.) To keep soil from washing into the watercourse, as well as to help prevent water leakage, you may want to build your edging up above the surrounding ground level. If runoff toward the watercourse is heavy, you may want to mortar between your edging stones for a better seal. Dense planting around the watercourse will also help prevent erosion and protect your pond water from pollution. For ideas about planting possibilities, take a look at moisture-loving perennials, grasses, and shrubs in "Adding Plants," page 94.

Camouflage. Plantings will blend the watercourse into the landscape.

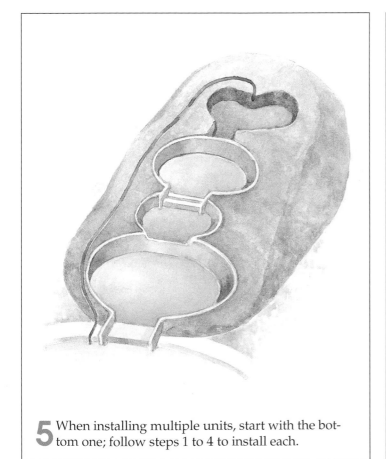

5 When installing multiple units, start with the bottom one; follow steps 1 to 4 to install each.

6 Place stones and plants around the unit to blend it into the landscape.

fountains & lights

A FOUNTAIN BRINGS YOUR LANDSCAPE TO LIFE
with movement and sound. Added to a pond, it breaks its reflected light into shimmering patterns. If you plan your fountain as you design your pond, you can take best advantage of your garden's exposure to capture sunlight in the spraying water. Fountains also enhance the aquatic life within your pond by adding oxygen to the water.

Choosing Fountains

You can find a fountain that's right for just about every type of garden design. To decide which type is best for you, consider not only sound, style, and size, but also the relationship to other landscape elements. If the fountain will be in your pond, you'll also need to keep in mind its effect on your plants and fish.

Sound is one of the greatest benefits of a fountain, adding music to your landscape and masking traffic and other noises. The effect can range from the creeklike burble of a low geyser to the high musical tinkle of a fine spray to the deeper, rainy-day resonance of a tall water column. Think about which type of sound will bring you the most enjoyment. Even on the smallest patio or in the tiniest yard, you can enjoy the soothing sounds of a fountain by installing a self-contained unit, a wall fountain that spills into a small basin, or a cobblestone reservoir

Spray or Statuary Fountains?

Choose a style that suits your landscape. Fountains of all styles come in two basic types: spray fountains (essentially just water nozzles, or jets, which spray water in different patterns) and statuary fountains, which spray water from a sculpture or figure of some type. Save the more elaborate spray patterns, and certainly fountains that incorporate classical statuary, for a formal design. In a pond that's informal but not meant to mimic nature, a simple spout or geyser will look the most appropriate. As a rule, fountains will look out of place in a wildlife pond, unless you choose a simple model that bubbles up from the surface like a natural spring.

Almost any spray-type fountain works with a modern-style home and pond; for statuary, look for a contemporary sculpture. For a bungalow or a farmhouse, an old water pump is the perfect accessory for a small pond.

Environmental Considerations

Also consider the overall shape of your pond. With a square or circular pond, fountains typically look best in the middle. If your pool is rectangular, you may want to install a line of pipes down the center spraying to the sides.

Look around and notice the shape of existing landscape elements, or envision shrubs or other large features you plan to add. You can complement the shape of nearby plants or garden furniture by choosing a fountain that has a vertical or rounded spray form, for example.

A classical fountain features a water nymph as its centerpiece, adding an elegant touch to this outdoor room.

The gentle trickle of water imitates the sound of spring rain as it lands on the base of this columnar fountain.

Wind Strength. Wind is also a factor that will affect the style of fountain that will work best in your garden. If you have a windy site, fountains that create a fine spray of droplets, or those that produce a thin film of water, such as a bell fountain, are unsuitable, as their pattern or symmetry will often be disturbed. If this is your situation, look for a geyser style that shoots up a heavy column of water.

Water Disturbance. If you want to grow floating or marginal plants, keep in mind how much the fountain will disturb the water surface of your pond. Water lilies and many other pond flora can't tolerate splashing or moving water; they'll need to be kept to the edge of the pond if you choose a tall, exuberant style of fountain. A low water column or the semispherical bell pattern will disturb the surface less than other designs would. If fish are more important to you than plants, however, choose a splashier fountain for more aeration.

Pond Size. The size of your pond will limit the size of your fountain. In a totally sheltered, windless garden, a fountain jet could be as high as the pond is wide, but this is a rare condition. A more common guideline is to make the height of your fountain no more than half the width or diameter of your pond to avoid drenching pondside benches, light fixtures, decks, patios—or you and your guests. Also, if the spray is too large for the size of the pond, the resulting water evaporation will lower the pond's water level.

Spray Fountains

A spray fountain consists of a nozzle or ring attached to the outlet pipe of a pump at or above the pond's water level. The simplest style is a length of vertical pipe run to a level just under the water surface, which provides a natural-looking geyser effect. Adding a narrow nozzle to the pipe will give you a taller, more dramatic geyser. Because geysers introduce air bubbles into the spray, they are especially good for aerating the water. (But size and place them carefully to avoid stirring up silt and sediment in the pond, which produces cloudy water.) To be visually effective, high, showy geysers require powerful, large-capacity pumps.

Most spray fountains are packaged as complete kits. Such kits include a molded plastic nozzle, the appropriate size pump, various fittings for installation, and a flow-control valve, which allows you to adjust spray height. Some kits contain several spray heads to change patterns. Others come with a tee fitting and diverter, which you'll need for attaching a second feature, such as a waterfall or filter. Before you assemble any of these components, be sure that your pump has the power for these add-ons.

You can also purchase a floating fountain that is ideal for short-term or periodic use. These relatively inexpensive spray fountains are designed with a built-in nozzle that attaches to an existing pump without plumbing (if your pump has an unused discharge valve).

Higher-quality nozzles can be disassembled to make cleaning the jet holes easier; lesser-quality nozzles are more difficult to clean. Brass nozzles are generally used for larger water displays, but they're more expensive than plastic. Keep in mind that nozzles with small holes clog easily and will require frequent cleaning. (Cleaning isn't a big production—just disassemble the nozzle, and hose it off or brush it with an old toothbrush.) Your nozzle will be less likely to clog if your pond also has a mechanical filter.

Far East Fountains

In a Japanese-style garden, you can create a simple bamboo spill fountain or the more complicated shishi odoshi (stag scarer). The simple bamboo fountain can be displayed in concert with a tsukubai, a basinlike stone used for washing one's hands and face in preparation for the Japanese tea ceremony. Set the stone basin on rocks so that water spills into it from the pipe and then spills over the edge onto the rocks before being recirculated. Instead of drawing its water from a reservoir, a shishi

The curved spray from a pair of spouting fish complements their rounded forms.

odoshi could substitute for a waterfall in a small stream; this device was originally used as a noisemaker to keep deer and other animals out of the garden. You can buy these deer-chaser features ready-made.

Instead of hooking your pump to a pipe and nozzle, attach the pump outlet to rubber tubing, and run the tubing through a bamboo pole. Be sure to hollow out all the bamboo "joints," so the tubing will easily pass through. (You may have to split the cane and glue it back together.) To join this vertical bamboo pipe and your spout at a slightly downward-facing angle, make an elbow joint with a block of wood or a short section of bamboo. Working from both sides, use a drill to create the angle.

Traditional elements in a Japanese water garden include a bamboo spill fountain called a tsukubai, left, and an ishidoro, or stone lantern, right.

Connecting a Spray Fountain

Installation is relatively simple but varies depending on the type of fountain, pump, and fittings. The easiest route to a spray fountain is to buy a complete kit and follow the instructions for assembling its components. The fittings either push or screw together, so the fountain can be easily constructed in just a few minutes.

On most submersible pumps designed for fountains, the water outlet is on top. This conveniently allows you to attach the rigid vertical PVC discharge pipe directly to the outlet. (You may need an adapter fitting on some units.) Cut the pipe to extend the required distance above the water level (typically 4 to 6 inches), and then simply attach the spray nozzle.

For pumps with a side discharge, you'll need to install an elbow fitting. To prevent the nozzle from clogging, buy a special prefilter or filter screen that attaches to the pump inlet. Some units combine the pump and filter in a single housing. The filter should be easily accessible for routine cleaning.

Once you've attached the fittings and spray nozzle according to the manufacturer's instructions, place the pump in the pond on a flat, level surface, such as a short stack of bricks. (Raising the pump off the bottom lessens the chances that it will get clogged with debris.) Both pump and discharge pipe must be firmly supported so that the pipe remains perfectly vertical.

If the unit has a tendency to tip or move around once it's running, place a few bricks along the sides of the pump to hold it in place. If it still tips, try a brick on top for more weight. Follow the guidelines given in "Electrical Requirements" on page 45 to provide the appropriate electrical connection for the pump.

Tools and Materials
- Saw (to cut PVC pipe)
- Adjustable wrench
- Necessary adapters
- PVC pipe (cut to length)
- Elbow fitting (for side discharge pumps)
- Prefilter or filter screen (if necessary)
- Bricks or prop material

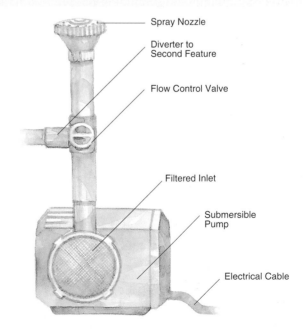

Spray Nozzle

Diverter to Second Feature

Flow Control Valve

Filtered Inlet

Submersible Pump

Electrical Cable

Spray Fountain. When buying a separate pump, be sure it's powerful enough for the fountain.

Statuary Fountains

Statuary fountains run the gamut of designs from classical Greek figures and wall-mounted gargoyles to sleek modern art forms and whimsical spouting frogs or fish. Most of those sold at garden and patio suppliers are precast concrete or cement and have a variety of surface finishes to simulate other materials, such as stone, alabaster, or bronze. Some suppliers also carry modern sculpture fountains of copper, brass, or bronze; most dealers can expand their offerings by ordering what you want from wholesale catalogs. In the past, fountain statuary was often made of lead. If you find one of these relics, be warned that lead can be toxic to fish and other aquatic creatures.

Statuary fountains are commonly sold as separate units, designed to be installed in the pond or next to it. You need to buy a pump to install with them, and a precast pedestal of the appropriate height on which to mount them. Other statuary fountains are complete, self-contained units with precast reservoir bowls and integrated, preplumbed pump/filter systems. These are designed to be stand-alone water features. Some are even small enough to fit on a tabletop.

How to Build a Cobblestone Reservoir

Here is a natural water feature that installs easily and requires no pond. It can be placed almost anywhere.

This simple water feature gives the illusion of a natural spring or geyser welling up and returning to the earth. It's a good stand-alone fountain if you don't want the hassle of maintaining a large pond. Even better, it makes a safe water feature for families with toddlers and small children.

The reservoir can go in a lawn or a flower bed or be sunk in a flagstone terrace. It can be as small as a dinner plate or a garden centerpiece 4 feet or more across; the vertical gusher fountains or bubblers usually used with these features can be adjusted to shoot water from 3 to 24 inches or higher, depending on the size pump you attach to them. Seek the advice of your water-garden supplier if you have any questions about buying the pump and fountain to match the desired size of your reservoir. As with any fountain, you need to have easy access to electrical power with a ground-fault circuit interrupter (GFCI).

Begin the installation by digging a hole in which to place the fountain assembly. You'll need a hole slightly larger than your plastic bucket or tub. Lower the bucket into the hole, and use a carpenter's level to make sure it is straight. Backfill the hole with soil, and create a bowl shape around it, sloping up.

Next, place the liner over the reservoir, and push the material down slightly into the bucket. Using scissors, cut a hole that's big enough to allow you to lower the pump to the bottom of the reservoir. Make sure the edges of the liner slope down toward the bucket; the liner needs to collect water from your fountain and return it to the bucket. Center the wire mesh over the lined reservoir, cutting a hole in the mesh large enough for the vertical pipe that connects to your fountain. Trim the pipe if needed so that it will be hidden by your stones.

To test the assembly, fill the bucket with water. Arrange stones around the fountain. A fountain kit with a flow adjuster will allow you to experiment with higher and lower geyser settings. When you are satisfied with the effect, arrange stones out to the edge of your liner, trimming off its corners.

Tools and Materials
- Shovel ■ Scissors ■ Spirit level
- Large plastic bucket, tub, or trash can reservoir
- Galvanized wire mesh (at least 5 inches larger than the diameter of the reservoir)
- Submersible pump
- Foaming gusher or bubbler spray-fountain kit
- Flexible pond liner (polyethylene is sturdy enough)
- Small, smooth pebbles or river rock (approx. 2 to 4 inches in diameter, or larger than the wire mesh)

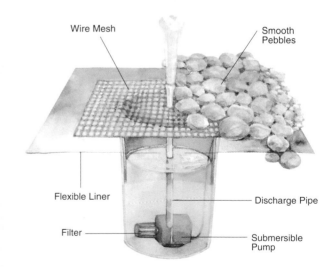

Wire Mesh   Smooth Pebbles

Flexible Liner   Discharge Pipe

Filter   Submersible Pump

Reservoir. This cobblestone reservoir is easy to assemble. It requires no pond and can be placed practically anywhere. Select smooth, matched stones bigger than the holes in the wire mesh.

Installing a Statuary Fountain

Most statuary fountains come with installation instructions. Use these in combination with the guidelines that follow to install the unit you've chosen. As with any moving water feature, you'll appreciate being able to turn the fountain on and off from indoors, so plug it into an outlet with an indoor switch. (See page 45 for guidelines on electrical installations.)

Self-Contained Fountains. This type of fountain includes a pump, a power cord, and all fittings. Typically, a small submersible pump sits in the statue pedestal, which sits in a reservoir bowl. Water spills from the fountain into the reservoir bowl, where it gets pumped back to the top. Units such as these can be placed anywhere within reach of a power supply. The pump cord runs from an overflow area inside the pedestal, down through a tube in the hollow base. Make sure the design of the unit you buy provides some way to gain access to the pump for cleaning and maintenance.

To install the fountain, simply set it on a sturdy, level base; fill it with water; and plug it in. Remember to check the water level frequently and refill the reservoir when needed; water can evaporate quickly from these shallow reservoirs. Follow the manufacturer's recommendations for regular care.

Wall Fountains. A wall fountain usually spills water through statuary—such as a mask or a decorative plaque—into a basin that hides a small pump. The statuary can be terra-cotta, plastic, fiberglass, cast concrete (often designed to mimic terra-cotta or stone), or metal. A stone water feature will be more expensive than one made of these other materials. Stone and cast-concrete wall fountains require a wall strong enough to support their weight, as well as sturdy, well-secured mounting hardware.

Wall fountains look best if the return pipe doesn't show. Thus the best place for these fountains is a freestanding wall that allows you to run the plumbing behind it. However, this is rarely practical for many of the situations where these small features work best, such as on a townhouse patio. Alternatives include hiding the tubing with vines or chiseling a vertical niche down the wall in which to run the tubing and then mortaring over it.

A more satisfactory option is to build out the wall using similar material—a new line of bricks, for instance, or an enclosure covered with clapboards to match your home's siding. Mount the fountain on the new surface, and run the pipe behind it.

If the fountain doesn't come with its own basin, home-made options range from building an elaborate brick or concrete reservoir to recycling a half barrel or an old sink or trough. Don't make the catch basin too small or rapid evaporation will necessitate frequent topping off. To keep splashing to a minimum, mount the fountain no higher above the catch basin than the diameter of the basin.

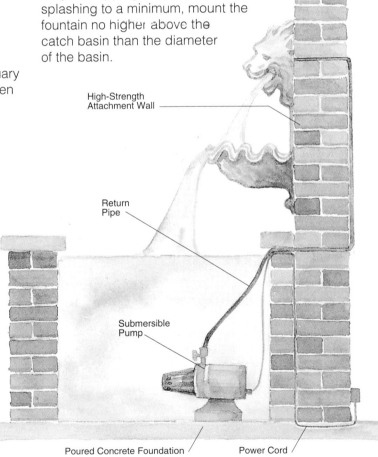

High-Strength Attachment Wall

Return Pipe

Submersible Pump

Poured Concrete Foundation

Power Cord

Statuary Fountains. Designs can be based on animals, characters from mythology, abstract sculpture, and the like.

Wall Fountain. Mount the fountain no higher above the catch basin than the diameter of the basin.

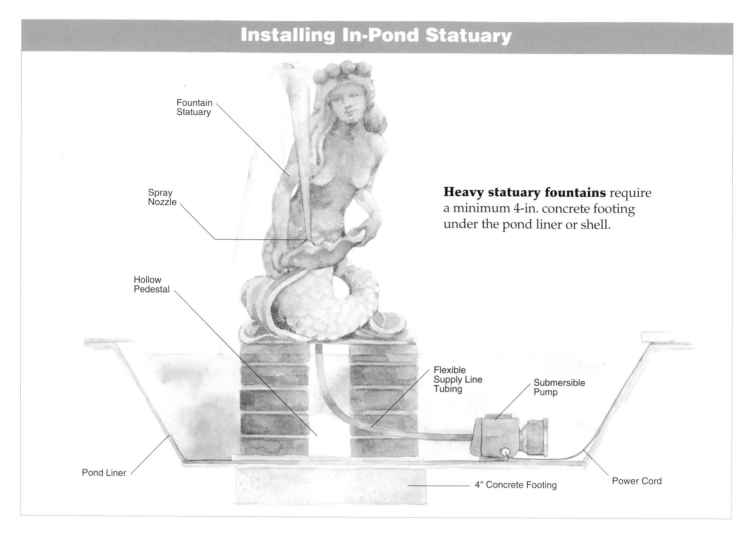

Fountain
Statuary

Spray
Nozzle

Heavy statuary fountains require a minimum 4-in. concrete footing under the pond liner or shell.

Hollow
Pedestal

Flexible
Supply Line
Tubing

Submersible
Pump

Pond Liner

4" Concrete Footing

Power Cord

In-Pond Statuary. The mechanics of installing fountain statuary in the pond are relatively straightforward. The hardest task is dealing with the weight of the statue. If it and its pedestal weigh more than 100 pounds, you'll need a concrete footing to support them before installing a flexible liner or preformed pond. On top of the liner or shell, mount the statue on a hollow in-pond pedestal. Or build your own pedestal with mortared bricks, stones, or other masonry. Then use flexible tubing to connect the pump to a supply pipe that projects from the statue's base.

The footing under the pond shell or liner should be a 4-inch-thick concrete subbase, a few inches wider and longer than the statue base or pedestal. If you forego a footing, the statue's weight may crack the rigid pond shell or tear the flexible pond liner. The footing must be smooth and level to give stable support; unless you have experience pouring concrete, hire a good contractor. For lighter statues, all you need to do is compact the soil firmly under the statue location with a tamper before installing the shell or liner. If you are unsure how firmly compacted the soil is, rent a powered compactor or a roller for this purpose. Once the shell or liner is installed, you're ready for the next step.

Protect flexible liners with a small piece of liner under-

layment under your pedestal. If you've purchased a pedestal, place it in the pond. If you haven't, build a pedestal by mortaring bricks or stones. Leave an opening near the bottom of the pedestal through which to run tubing from the pump to the statue. Use a spirit level to check your work as you build up the height of the pedestal, as the top needs to be absolutely level. (If you have doubts about your handiwork or are installing a valuable statue, hire an experienced contractor.) To facilitate cleaning and other maintenance chores, leave the pump outside the pedestal. Situate it as close to the pedestal as possible, and then run flexible tubing from the pump up through the pedestal into the statue. Be sure that you allow enough tubing at the top to connect easily to the statue.

With a helper, move the statue into position on the pedestal. While your helper tilts the statue slightly, reach underneath to make the connection between the pump outlet tubing and the pipe projecting from the statue's base. (You may need an adapter fitting. Check before you have the statue in place.) Secure the connection with a hose clamp, and then rest the statue in its final position. Don't mortar or otherwise attach the statue to the pedestal—you may need to replace the outlet tubing later.

Lighting

When you consider ways to illuminate your pond at night, underwater lights may seem like the obvious choice, and some fountain systems come equipped with them. When well placed in clear water, underwater lights can highlight water lilies, waterfalls, and other features. But poorly placed underwater lights create glare. They also eliminate pond reflections of the moon or of garden features you highlight with aboveground lights.

A few lights well positioned in the landscape around a water feature are generally more effective than underwater lights. You can create dramatic nighttime reflections by directing hidden, ground-level spotlights up toward surrounding trees or tall shrubs. Waterfalls or fountains will sparkle when you direct lights toward them from the pond edges. Keep it simple: generally, a few well-placed spotlights or accent lights will produce a more desirable effect than strong floodlights that light up the entire yard. Spend time moving the light fixtures around from one location to another until you are satisfied.

Consider using lighting for safety reasons, like illuminating walkways or steps to the pond. Low-level, ornamental downlighting fixtures placed knee-high at intervals along the borders of a walk or attached to step railings provide enough illumination to define walkways without over-lighting.

Nightime Water Views. Carefully selecting sites for aboveground light fixtures lets you highlight rocks, waterfalls, trees, and pondside planting areas to create extra excitement (top).

Low-Voltage Illumination. Lighting around your water feature invites viewing at any time and helps ensure the safety of visitors (left, top and bottom).

In-Pond Fixture Types

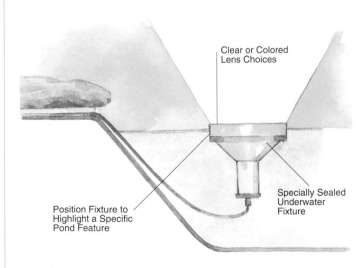

Clear or Colored Lens Choices

Position Fixture to Highlight a Specific Pond Feature

Specially Sealed Underwater Fixture

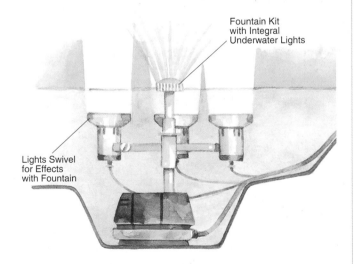

Fountain Kit with Integral Underwater Lights

Lights Swivel for Effects with Fountain

Fixture Kit. Many lighting suppliers now offer fixture kits. A low-voltage (12-volt) system is less expensive to buy and easier to install than a standard 120-volt system.

Underwater Lighting. This can be dramatic and eye-catching, but easily overdone. It's best to go slowly and start simply. Low-voltage systems are the safest and easiest to install.

chapter 6
bridges

BRIDGES AND STEPPING-STONES provide a way to cross a pond or stream. But they also let you enjoy the pond from a different viewpoint and give you better access for maintenance. For the best results, plan them while you are designing your pond rather than trying to add them later. You may need a permit to install a bridge. Ask your local building inspector about codes.

Wooden Bridges

Wooden bridges can be as simple as a weathered plank across a stream or as ornate as a lacquered Japanese "camelback." They add architectural interest and direct the flow of traffic in the garden. A bridge just plunked down across the water detracts from the charm of your pond. Give viewers a reason to get to the other side, such as a bench, a garden ornament, or interesting plants.

Size the bridge so that it is in proportion with the pond or stream in length, width, and height. Make the bridge wide enough to cross easily and safely; 2 feet is the narrowest you should consider. For a very narrow stream or a small natural pond, a couple of wide, sturdy planks laid from one bank to the other may suffice. Bridges more than 12 to 18 inches above the water surface will need handrails, both for safety and for aesthetics. Be sure to provide a sturdy foundation for the support posts when you build a bridge of any size. If you plan to build a bridge with a span longer than 8 feet, you may want to consult a building contractor, because bridges of this size will require larger beams, additional supports, or both.

In buying material to build your bridge (or working with a contractor), specify the use of pressure-treated lumber, as well as corrosion-resistant hardware and fasteners. Lumber that is used at or near the ground should be rated for ground or soil contact. Any wood that will be in regular contact with water, such as the mid-span support for a bridge longer than 8 feet, you will need to use treated lumber that is rated for marine or seawall use. However, you should avoid using wood treated with creosote or penta-chlorophenol, both of which are toxic to fish and plants. (If you have any treated lumber left over from your project, remember that it is not safe for burning in the fireplace. Check with your lumber supplier or your county sanitation department for specific guidance on how to properly dispose of it.)

If you've decided that a bridge is appropriate for your pond but aren't sure how to go about designing one, you will find the plans to build one described on the next few pages.

You can build a simple footbridge across your pond with doubled 2x8s for support beams, 2x6s for decking and handrails, and 4x4s for the posts. Use pressure-treated lumber and galvanized carriage bolts and nails. The following instructions are for a 5-foot-wide bridge that can span a pond or stream up to 6 feet across.

Crossings. You can purchase a prefabricated bridge if you don't want to build it yourself. First, check with the local building inspector.

Natural Bridge. Massive stone slabs make ideal stepping-stones or a bridge. If you can handle their sheer weight and bulk, you can build this style of bridge quickly.

Adding a Footbridge

1 Make the Support Beams. Each of the three beams is made with two 2x8s nailed together. Most long boards have a slight crown, as shown in the illustration. You can best determine which edge is crowned by looking down the length of each board. Attach and install the boards with the crowns facing up.

Make sure that the boards are all the same length; trim if necessary. Stack two 2x8s on top of each other, align the edges, and fasten with 8d nails, about 10 on each side, spaced and staggered as shown.

2 Position the Posts. Place three 4x4 posts on each side of the pond, stream, or depression. Extend the posts 1 foot above grade. For a bridge with a railing, ex-tend the four corner posts at least 4 feet above grade. Center the two sets of posts no more than 7 feet apart. Measuring from the center of the middle post on each side, set one corner post 2 feet on center and the other 2 feet 6½ inches on center.

Stake the locations of the posts. Then dig 8-inch-diam-eter postholes at least 6 inches below the frost line. If frost is not a problem in your area, dig the holes at least 30 inches deep. Add 6 inches of gravel. Tamp the gravel.

Center the 4x4 posts in each hole. Brace the posts so that they are plumb. Mix and pour concrete an inch or so above grade at the support posts. Tamp the concrete with a piece of wood so that it completely surrounds each post. Slope the concrete away from the posts for good drainage. Let the concrete cure completely.

Tools & Materials

- Measuring tape
- Circular saw
- Hammer
- Mortar hoe
- Wheelbarrow or mortar pan
- Spirit level
- Drill, ⅝-inch spade bit, ½-inch spade bit (for optional handrail)
- Wrench
- Portable saber saw
- Power sander
- Six 8-foot 2x8s
- Six 4x4s (length depends on depth of postholes and handrail)
- Nine 10-foot 2x6s
- Two 8-foot 2x6s (for optional handrail)
- 1 cubic foot gravel
- Concrete (amount depends on depth of postholes)
- Six 20d common nails
- 3 pounds 10d galvanized common nails
- 1 pound 8d galvanized common nails
- Twelve ½ x 7½-inch carriage bolts, nuts, washers
- Eight ⅜ x 6-inch carriage bolts, nuts, washers (for optional handrail)

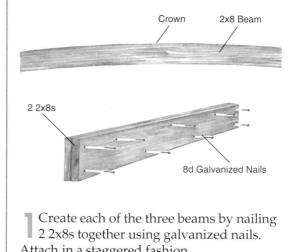

1 Create each of the three beams by nailing 2 2x8s together using galvanized nails. Attach in a staggered fashion.

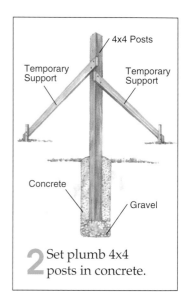

2 Set plumb 4x4 posts in concrete.

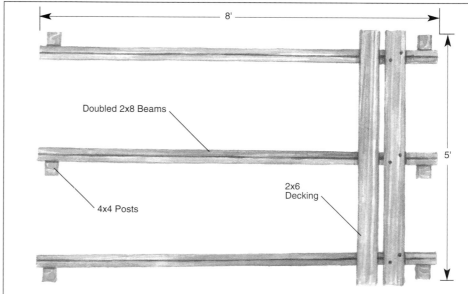

3 Secure the beams to the posts using carriage bolts. Cut 10-ft.-long 2x6s in half, and attach to beams, leaving a ¼-in. space between decking.

3 Install the Beams and Decking. Set the beams against the posts. Study the illustration opposite bottom for proper beam placement. The two outside beams should be installed on the insides of the corner posts. Align the beams so that they overhang the posts equally on both sides of the bridge. Check the beams for level in both directions using a spirit level. For temporary support, attach the beams with one 20d nail into each post. With the beams leveled and temporarily attached to the posts, trim the posts flush with the tops of the beams. (Do not, however, trim the corner posts if you are installing a handrail.)

Secure the beams. At each post, drill two ⅝-inch holes through the posts and beams. Secure the beams to the posts permanently with ½-inch-diameter, 7½-inch-long carriage bolts, nuts, and washers.

Cut the 10-foot-long 2x6s in half. Fasten the decking across the tops of the beams with 10d nails. The decking should overlap the outside beams by about 4½ inches on each side. Keep the decking square by starting at one end, installing the first 2x6 flush with the ends of the beams. Leave a ¼-inch gap between each board.

Stepping-Stones

If you want to provide a means for crossing your pond or stream without blocking the view or adding a vertical element to the landscape, add stepping-stones to the water feature. For formal ponds, use square or rectangular concrete slabs, large quarry tiles, or cut stone. For an informal look, use irregularly shaped flat rocks or flagstones.

For safety, place large stones on some sort of footing

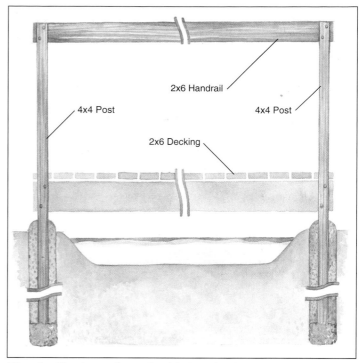

Handrails. A single or double handrail provides an extra measure of safety for bridge crossers. (The local building code may require one and specify how it is to be constructed.) Use 2x6 lumber for the handrails.

or pier, such as those shown below. If your water feature contains either a flexible liner or preformed shell, you will need to pour the footing before installing the liner. Protect the liner by installing layers of pond-liner underlayment. Place one layer between the footing and the liner and another between the liner and the pier or stepping-stone.

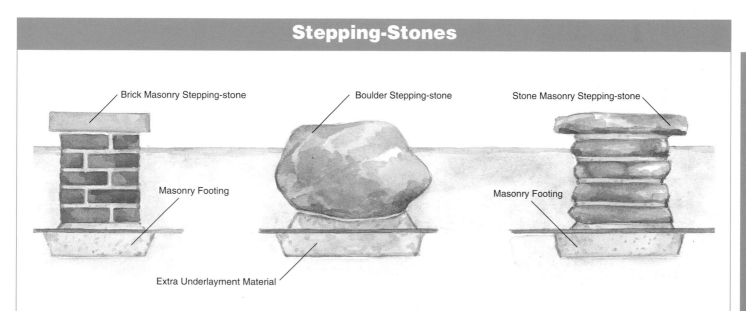

Stepping-Stones

Brick Masonry Stepping-stone

Boulder Stepping-stone

Stone Masonry Stepping-stone

Masonry Footing

Masonry Footing

Extra Underlayment Material

A variety of materials may be used for pond stepping-stones: brick, large flat boulders, flat stones, quarry tiles, and concrete slabs. A stable footing should be placed under each one.

water quality

KEEPING POND WATER CLEAR AND HEALTHY for fish and plants also makes it more attractive to humans. Achieving the proper balance is one of the greatest challenges in water gardening. Clear shouldn't mean crystal clear, which looks unnatural. Also, water that's crystal clear may still contain chemical and mineral pollutants, while slightly brown or green water may be ideal for pond life.

A Pond's Life

Factors that affect the ecological balance of your pond include its size and depth, the amount of sun it receives, water temperature and movement, pollutants from runoff, and the kind and number of plants and fish you have. Because of this complicated ecological interplay, your pond can take anywhere from several weeks to several months to achieve an ideal balance. Then the pond can stay balanced indefinitely unless any of these factors changes appreciably.

How Your Pond Works

Your pond or water garden is a small, self-contained ecosystem. When you introduce aquatic plants, they draw nutrients (especially nitrates and phosphates) from the water and, if they're potted, also from the soil. These nutrients, combined with sunlight, are what nourish plants, enabling them to grow and thereby release oxygen into the water as a result of photosynthesis.

When fish are introduced into this ecosystem, they consume the oxygen produced by the plants. Fish also derive other benefits from plants. Surface plants such as water lilies help keep water from overheating by providing shade from the hot summer sun. Plants also give fish a place to hide from other fish, cats, raccoons, birds, and other predators.

In turn, fish provide gases and nutrients that plants need in order to grow: carbon dioxide from their breathing, and nitrogen and other chemicals from their wastes. Fish also help control populations of plant-eating insects. To some measure, they likewise consume some of the plants and thus keep excessive plant growth in check.

When the numbers of fish and plants in the pond reach a stable relationship (not too many of one or the other), the pond is in biological balance. The reason balanced ponds are relatively clear is because plants and fish in tandem help control the algal growth that can turn the water cloudy. Scavengers such as snails and tadpoles also help balance the pond by consuming algae and organic debris.

Water Problems. The most common water problems are caused by having too many fish or feeding the fish too much. A buildup of dead plant material, having too many living plants covering the surface, prolonged hot weather, or an excess of algae can deplete oxygen and lead to more problems. Your water may also contain pollutants from pond-building materials and toxic chemicals that may have been washed or blown into the water from outside sources.

A healthy pond is a self-contained ecosystem in which water, plants, and aquatic life depend upon each other for their survival.

Incorporating a waterfall or a fountain in your pond design will promote good water quality. Either of these features will aerate your pond and help ensure that fish have all the oxygen they need. Lack of oxygen will bring fish to the surface, in search of oxygen absorbed from the air. This sometimes happens with little warning after long periods of hot, dry weather. But it can also occur in stormy weather, when water may turn and decrease available oxygen in the pond's top layer, or when prolonged cloudy weather disrupts photosynthesis by your pond's plants. You can rescue gasping fish quickly by oxygenating the pond with spray from a garden hose. Or you can have on hand a separate aeration kit that includes an air pump. If the need for aeration arises, you simply place the pump about an inch below the water surface, screening the pump's intake so that it doesn't suck in small fish or other tiny pond creatures while in operation. When fish behavior returns to normal, these measures can be discontinued.

Controlling Algae

When you first fill your pond, the water will be crystal clear. After a few days, however, the water will turn murky and take on a greenish tinge. This is caused by microscopic, single-celled, free-floating algae. Their presence is to be expected until aquatic plants have established themselves. Submerged (oxygenating) plants eventually starve the algae by outcompeting them for available nutrients. Floating plants and water lilies likewise help starve the algae; they not only consume nutrients but cut off the sunlight that algae need to grow. To a lesser degree, fish, snails, and accidentally-introduced algae eaters such as water fleas also help.

Algal Concentration. You can expect to have some algae in the pond, even after it's balanced. At a level that causes only a slight discoloration, algae are not harmful to fish or plants; they help conceal the artificial-looking liner or shell as well as any planters or pump on the pond bottom. As the pond matures, most of the free-floating algae will eventually be replaced by visible forms of filamentous, mossy, and slime algae growing on the sides and bottom of the pond, as well as on plants, rocks, and any other convenient surface.

When algal growth becomes excessive, however, it's worse than unsightly. Not only do algae consume the pond's oxygen in the process of decaying, but in excessive amounts they will cut off sunlight to oxygenating plants below the surface, reducing the oxygen supply even further. Algae can also coat the floating leaves of water lilies and other plants so that they lose their ability to help balance pond gases. When pond water is depleted of oxygen, fish begin to die.

Natural Control. Make every effort to control algae both naturally—with oxygenating plants and pond scavengers such as tadpoles and snails—and mechanically. Algae that forms a scummy mat on the surface, sometimes called filamentous algae, can be removed with a fine-mesh net or by twirling it around a long-handled brush or rake as you would twirl spaghetti on a fork.

Chemical Control. You can buy chemicals called algicides to kill algae. Many people use algicides for initial algal control after they install a pond or to control the algal blooms that tend to occur in spring. But like any garden chemical, algicides are just a temporary remedy and not a cure. Moreover, they can cause other problems. Some algicides are toxic to fish, and those sold in pet stores for use in aquariums, in particular, will affect the growth of other water plants. (Always check the package label.) Furthermore, these products do not guard against the growth of new algae, which is inevitable. A much better, long-term solution, in addition to the natural controls mentioned above, is adding one or more filters to your system. (See "Filtration" on page 73.) If algal growth continues to be a problem even after some type of filtration has been installed, consult a pond specialist.

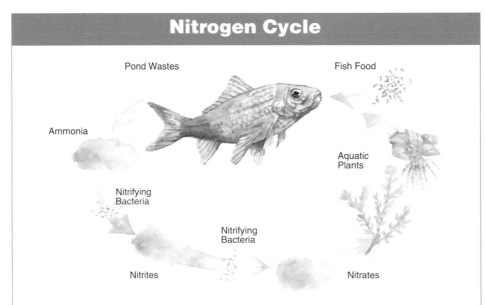

Nitrogen Cycle

Pond Wastes

Fish Food

Ammonia

Aquatic Plants

Nitrifying Bacteria

Nitrifying Bacteria

Nitrites

Nitrates

Nitrogen Cycle. Ammonia from pond wastes can be fatal to fish. Bacteria in biological filters and some algae convert ammonia first to nitrites (also harmful), then to nitrates that plants can consume.

Balancing a New Pond

Once you've done all the hard work to install your pond, you'll be eager to populate it with plants and fish. But a bit of patience now will pay off with fewer problems later. Do your homework by calling the local water authorities so that you will know what chemicals your municipal water supply contains. You can also obtain test kits and any chemicals you will need to correct chlorination or any other anticipated imbalances. (See "What's in Your Water" on page 72.) The steps that follow will help you create a natural biological balance in your brand-new pond.

Rinse and Fill the Pond. If you've used pool paints, wood stains or preservatives, pipe-joint glues, or similar wet materials on your pond, let them dry thoroughly, because otherwise they can contaminate pond water, and poison fish and plants. Treat mortar, concrete, and cement with an acidic solution to prevent lime from leaching out of these materials; this would make the pond water too alkaline for animal and plant life. (See "Constructing a Lined In-Ground Pond," Step 6 on page 32.) After you've rinsed the solution off, drained the water, and rinsed out any debris remaining from pond construction, fill the pond with fresh water. If you've installed a filter, run it continuously for the first few days before introducing plants. Depending on your situation, you may have to drain and refill your pond several times.

Test the Water. When you first fill the pond, the water may contain chemicals and minerals that are toxic to fish and plants. Well water may contain hydrogen sulfide, which is also produced by decaying organic matter, and detectable by its slight rotten-egg smell. If this compound is present in your pond water, it will require extra aeration. Tap water from public supply systems may contain chlorine, chlorine dioxide, chloramine, or ammonia; well water won't. Allowing tap water to stand for a few days will get rid of most free chlorine, but chlorine dioxide and chloramine require chemical treatment.

Test the water after filling the pond but before introducing plants or fish. You can buy kits from pond dealers, garden suppliers, and pet shops to test for most problems. The kits usually include instructions for correcting any problems you find. Some pond dealers and pet shops provide water-testing services and can advise you on proper treatment.

Algae Removal. Excess algae is unsightly and unhealthy for your pond. It is easily removed with a stick, rake, or long-handled brush.

Adjust Water Conditions. Follow instructions included with the test kits to correct any problems that have been detected. Some fish and plant dealers recommend giving the pond a dose of a general-purpose water conditioner before adding fish or plants, as an added safety measure. But just as you shouldn't use chemicals in the rest of your garden unless there's a good reason, you shouldn't use water conditioners in your pond unless tests show that they're actually needed. Even if you use a conditioner to achieve your initial water balance, try to determine the source of the pollution to prevent future problems.

Introduce Plants. Once water tests show that you've removed chloramines and other levels are within a safe range—and the danger of frost is past—you can add plants. The sooner you add them, the sooner they can help to prevent algal buildup and provide oxygen and food for fish. The pond water will likely start to turn green right then, but it will probably clear up in a few weeks as plants become established.

Introduce Fish. Two to three weeks after you've introduced plants, it's safe to add fish, snails, and tadpoles. The size and quantity of plants and fish a pond will support depends on the water quality and the available oxygen and sunlight. A pond with good water circulation and filtration will support a larger population of fish than a stagnant pond without a filter.

Algae: Fascinating and Sometimes Helpful

Algae may look unappealing in your pond, but they can be beautiful under a microscope. Under magnification, their usual colors of green, brown, and yellow can give way to reds, blues, oranges, and other hues.

Algae lack flowers and the leaves, stems, and roots that circulate nutrients in "higher" plants. They range from the single-celled forms that can cloud your pond to sea-dwelling kelp more than 200 feet long. The type that turns a pond murky is called planktonic, a term that covers all forms that are suspended in water. Under a microscope, you would see that these algae have threadlike "tails" (flagella) that allow them to move through the water.

Planktonic algae thrive when it's warm and sunny. When the weather cools in fall, you might see more filamentous algae—the type that forms long, hairy-looking strands. Some of these algae are yellow or gold. Spirogyra, the melodic name of which derives from its spiral bands of chlorophyll, consists of long strings of cells that attach themselves to the pond bottom and other surfaces.

Not all algae live in ponds. One called Haematococcus prefers shallow water such as birdbaths. (You might see its telltale reddish color if you have the Japanese water basin called a tsukubai.) Others grow on moist stones or even in soil. Some of these soil dwellers are the blue-green algae, or cyanobacteria, that have become such a popular item in many health-food stores.

Mosslike algae that grow on the side of the pond are beneficial and a sign of good pond health. Because they harbor the same kind of bacteria found in an artificial biological filter, they help to remove toxic chemicals from your water.

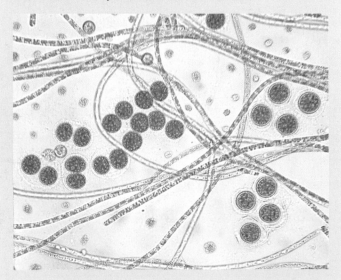

What's in Your Water?

Water-garden suppliers offer kits you can use to test water for potentially harmful chemicals or unhealthy situations. Here's a quick explanation of what you might find.

- **Ammonia.** Ammonia is present in fish waste, so the usual explanation for high levels of ammonia is having too many fish. But some public water supplies contain ammonia if they've been treated with chloramines. Decaying organic matter will also contribute to ammonia levels. Ammonia will stress your fish, and too much will kill them. Clean out the pond bottom, and change at least 50 percent of the water. The best control for an ongoing problem with excess ammonia is having a biological filter installed.

- **Chlorine.** This chemical is the most common additive in municipal water supplies and fortunately is the easiest to deal with, as it dissipates within 24 to 48 hours. If you are adding chlorinated water to an existing pond, however, avoid adding more than 20 percent of the pond volume at one time to keep from harming the fish.

- **Chloramine.** This is another additive used to purify municipal water supplies. A combination of chlorine and ammonia, it's more toxic to fish than chlorine and doesn't dissipate on standing. Find out from local water suppliers whether it's used in your tap water. If so, always have on hand the chemicals needed to neutralize it.

- **Nitrites.** These chemicals result from the breakdown of ammonia and so are most likely to be present when there are too many fish, and they can suffocate fish. Control nitrites by changing half the water and treating it with 2½ pounds of dissolved pond salt per 100 gallons of water. (Dissolve the salt in a small amount of water first, and remove as many plants as possible.) You can make emergency filters by putting an absorbent substance called zeolite, sold by water suppliers, into mesh bags and dragging this around the pond.

- **Nitrates.** These are harmless compounds that result from the breakdown of ammonia or nitrites; they serve as nutrients for plants. Their presence can show that your pond is going through a healthy process of converting those harmful compounds into the harmless form that plants can use. An excess of these nutrients can feed algae, however, and may indicate the need for more submerged plants (oxygenators) and other plants. In general, you won't need to test for nitrates.

- **pH.** Short for "potential hydrogen," pH is a measure of acidity or alkalinity. The scale ranges from 1.0 (highly acidic) to 14.0 (highly alkaline), with 7.0 being neutral. Healthy pond water ranges in pH from 6.5 to 8.5. Tap water is more likely to be within this range than well water in some areas. Alkaline water can be caused by leaching from concrete or limestone rocks; fish tend to raise acidity. You can buy commercial products to adjust your pond water's pH, but use them carefully because a rapid change in pH is harmful to fish.

- **Hardness.** Hard water, which has an excess of minerals, is not in itself harmful, but it can affect pH. If your tap water is hard, it may be alkaline; if your tap water is very soft, it's probably somewhat acidic. While there are kits available for testing hardness, you won't need them. If you suspect hard or soft water, just test the pH.
- **Oxygen.** Maintaining high levels of oxygen in your pond keeps everything in balance. You might want to test for dissolved oxygen before adding fish or if the fish you have seem ill. If oxygen levels test low and you already have a waterfall or a fountain, add an aerating device to provide more oxygen. Oxygen can be depleted by having too many fish.

Filtration

If your goal is to have a small ornamental pond with a few plants and fish and you don't mind slightly cloudy water from time to time, you may not need a filter. If, however, you have a large pond with many fish and want clear water for viewing them, a good filter will certainly help. Koi ponds especially need clear, relatively pure water.

There are two basic types of filters: mechanical and biological. Mechanical filters trap algae and other particles, while biological filters convert chemical pollutants into harmless substances. When you're shopping for any type of filter, it's a good idea to seek out the advice of an independent dealer who carries several brand names.

Filters require pumps to move water through them. If the pump will be used for filtration only (and not also for a waterfall or fountain), arrange the system so that the pump intake is at one end of the pond—preferably the deepest—and the discharge is at the other. This will pro-duce a slight current across the bottom of the pond, which will aid in recirculating the water to remove sediment and other water impurities.

Mechanical Filters

Don't confuse mechanical filters with the filter screens and prefilters attached to pumps. Those screens are meant only to keep debris from clogging the pump impeller and fountain jets; they won't have any effect on water quality. Debris- or algae-filled water will be hard on your pump, however. (And a good mechanical filter will keep the screen or prefilter from clogging with algae.)

The primary purpose of a mechanical filter is to trap large particles of suspended matter that can cloud water. This material includes fish wastes, decaying organic matter, floating algae, and leftover fish food. Mechanical filters are less expensive than biological filters, and they start filtering your pond immediately, whereas biological filters are not effective for several weeks. Their main drawback is that they require frequent cleaning—at least once a week, and usually daily during the summer.

Some mechanical filters (suction filters) are plumbed into the pump inlet, while others (pressure filters) are plumbed to the pump outlet. Some go inside the pond, and others are placed outside. An in-pond cartridge-type filter is sufficient for most small ponds (those with a capacity of less than 1,000 gallons). These devices use a corrugated polyester filter medium, which looks and works much like an automobile oil filter. Other small filters strain the debris through screens, foam, or woven fiber pads or wraps. Some let you add activated charcoal or a mineral called zeolite to remove ammonia and other chemical impurities from the water. The effectiveness of any filter depends primarily on its overall size, which is usually expressed as the surface area of the filter medium (in square feet) and the amount of water pumped through it (in gallons per hour). Manufacturers generally provide performance capacities for their filters—for example, "for ponds up to 300 gallons."

Stocking Formula for a Balanced Pond

It will take time and experimentation to achieve a balance between plant and animal life. For starters, use the following formulas for stocking your pond with plants, fish, and snails.

- Two bunches of submerged (oxygenating) plants per square yard of pond surface.
- One medium to large water lily for each square yard of surface area, or enough water lilies, lotuses, or floating plants to cover 50 to 70 percent of the pond surface during the summer months. Most water plants go dormant during the winter and then reestablish themselves in spring. Once established, water lilies and other water plants will occasionally need to be divided or pruned to prevent overcrowding.

- Two inches of fish (length) for each square foot of pond surface in a pond 18 to 24 inches deep, or one koi for every 25 square feet in pond surface. Keep in mind their eventual size and rate of growth, as well as the possibility that they will produce fry.
- Eight to ten small snails or six to eight large snails per square yard of pond surface.

Skimmer. This device removes leaves and other large debris before they fall to the pond bottom and start decomposing.

Very large ponds (1,000 gallons or more) require more substantial filters. Options include a diatomaceous-earth filter or a high-rate sand filter, similar to those used in swimming pools. These large filters must be placed outside the pond and require a large pump and extensive plumbing.

Skimmers. A variation on the mechanical filter, called a skimmer, removes debris before it can sink to the bottom of the pond, holding it in a bag, much like a vacuum cleaner bag, that you remove a couple of times a month. Water gardeners with numerous deciduous trees find them indispensable. Skimmers are installed in the ground at the perimeter of the pond. Dealers recommend that they be run with a separate pump so that all of the water, not just that on the surface, is circulated regularly.

To be effective, a mechanical filter needs a high flow rate. The filter should be combined with a pump that can circulate all the water in the pond once every two hours. If you've installed a fountain or waterfall, be sure you have a pump large enough to operate that feature and still provide sufficient circulation through the filter. Your water-garden dealer can advise you. If your budget allows, select a filter that exceeds the minimum requirements for your pond. The larger the filter, the less often you'll have to clean it. Fortunately, cleaning generally takes only a few minutes: you simply remove the filter pad, cartridge, or screen, and wash it off with a garden hose.

Biological Filters

The main function of these filters is not to remove debris or even algae but to convert organic pollutants into relatively benign substances. Primarily, this means converting ammonia from fish wastes (and to a lesser extent, from decaying plant matter and uneaten fish food) into nitrates, which can be absorbed by plants as a nutrient. If you

have an excess of nitrates, however, you are more likely to have algae. To avoid this situation, be sure to include a sufficient number of oxygenating (submerged) plants. (See page 98 for descriptions.) They are particularly good at absorbing nitrates.

How They Work. Biological filters contain two or more layers of gravel or other medium that harbor large concentrations of beneficial nitrifying bacteria naturally found in ponds. As water slowly flows through the medium, these bacteria break down toxic ammonia (and nitrites, which result from the partial breakdown of ammonia) into nitrates. Other specialized microorganisms feast on single-celled algae passing through the filter. More-complex types of biological filters may incorporate mechanical pre-filters or compartments filled with activated charcoal, zeolites, or other media.

Look for a filter that includes an aeration tower, which provides additional oxygen for beneficial bacteria. Dirty water is pumped from the pond through the aeration tower to the bottom of the filter, where it slowly percolates up through the gravel filter medium (giving the bacteria a chance to eat their fill). It exits near the top of the filter and through a return pipe to the pond. (The return pipe can be hooked up to a waterfall.)

You can grow submerged plants in the top layer of gravel to provide additional oxygen for the bacteria and to absorb nutrients. The layers of gravel also serve as a crude mechanical filter to trap some suspended particles in the water, further clarifying it. If you still have problems with debris, add a mechanical filter to the filtering system.

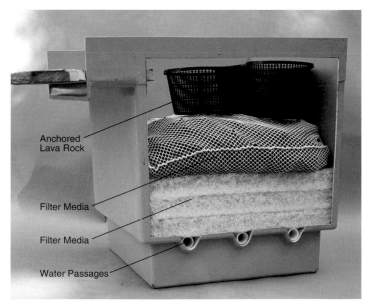

Anchored Lava Rock

Filter Media

Filter Media

Water Passages

Waterfall Box and Biological Filter. This upflow biological filter is used to convert organic wastes into nontoxic forms. As water flows through various media, substances like ammonia are broken down and rendered harmless.

Cleaning. About once a month, drain the filter by opening a drain valve at the bottom to remove accumulated silt and sediment. (You can use this to fertilize garden beds.) Then lightly rinse the filter medium to dislodge trapped particles. Don't use heavy sprays of chlorinated tap water, as that would tend to dislodge or even kill the beneficial bacteria in the filter medium; a small bucketful of rainwater is better. Give the filter a more thorough cleaning at the end of the season. (The bacteria won't survive below 55°F anyway, so once it gets cold, you don't have to worry about chlorinated water.)

Unlike mechanical filters, biological filters do not require a high flow rate to operate efficiently. The pump needs to turn over the total water volume only once every four to six hours. So even though biological filters are initially more expensive than mechanical filters, they are less expensive to run because they use less electricity.

Biological filters need to be run constantly and don't start working efficiently until several weeks after they are installed—unless you give them a dose of "starter" bacteria, purchased from your water-garden supplier. Most of them are large, unsightly tanks placed outside the pond above water level and will need to be disguised somehow, such as behind a shed or under a deck. Several manufacturers have recently introduced small in-pond biological filters, but their capacity is limited to ponds of 300 gallons or less.

Other Water-Cleaning Devices

Mechanical and biological filters will be sufficient for most ponds. Where algae or fish diseases are an ongoing problem, consider adding one or more of the following devices.

Ultraviolet Sterilizers. Ultraviolet (UV) water sterilizers are sometimes used in conjunction with a biological filter. Plumbed into the inlet side of the filter, these units consist of an ultraviolet bulb encased in a transparent, waterproof sleeve, which in turn is placed inside a tube plumbed into the system. When microscopic organisms are exposed to concentrated ultraviolet light, the UV energy causes the cell content (protoplasm) of the microorganisms to explode. Algae, bacteria, viruses, and certain fish parasites can be killed in this manner. The light also encourages minute organic particles to clump together so that they can be trapped in the filter. UV sterilizers usually aren't needed if you have a good biological filter. But if you're constantly dealing with fish diseases or parasites, they may help.

Ozone Generators. These devices purify water and reduce bacteria and fish parasites. They convert oxygen from the air into ozone and infuse it into the water, where it breaks down chloramines, ammonia, nitrites, and phosphates into harmless gases that escape the pond. Like UV light, ozone promotes the clumping of minute toxic

Natural Filter. Clean your pond the way that nature intended, using plants to remove excess nutrients from the water.

waste particles so that they are more easily trapped by other filters. Used for many years to sterilize water in swimming pools and spas, ozone generators are becoming popular among koi hobbyists. Although they are costly, they may be a good investment if you want a crystal-clear fishpond with few or no plants to remove nitrates from your water.

Natural Plant Filters. These are, ironically, another option for ponds with few or no plants. The filter is nothing more than a separate small pond or a large tub densely planted with such plants as water hawthorn, watercress, water lettuce, or water hyacinth placed between the filter outlet and the main pond. Because the plants consume nitrates and other nutrients produced by the biological filter, they reduce the algal growth in the main pond. They can also be incorporated as an attractive part of the overall landscape design. The expense of ultraviolet sterilizers and ozone generators probably can't be justified unless you are raising valuable fish. Using natural plant filters to remove excess nutrients is a low-tech, relatively inexpensive option.

maintenance

ONCE YOUR POND IS ESTABLISHED, you'll need to clean and maintain it on a continual basis. But caring for a pond isn't the drudgery you may think. There are many time-saving devices available. Pond maintenance can actually be a pleasurable pastime that puts you in touch with the plants and animals that live in your water garden.

Routine Seasonal Tasks

Maintaining a clean, healthy pond is a cross between keeping up a garden and caring for an aquarium. Even during the summer months, when your pond requires the most attention, it shouldn't take you more than an hour or two every week to keep it in prime condition.

Like the rest of your garden, your pond will go through seasonal cycles. But while residents of temperate climates can almost forget their perennial beds for a few months during winter, they need to be vigilant year-round when it comes to their ponds.

The sequence of routine maintenance tasks is the same everywhere, even though spring comes sooner to North Carolina than Vermont.

Spring

The advent of warmer weather is a time for inspection and remediation. Early spring, before plants have leafed out, is a good time to check your pond's edges for any settling or shifting and repair them if needed. Grounds softened (but not soggy) by spring rain make landscaping easier. Check your electrical connections, lights, and pumps; repair any loose connections. Make sure ground-fault circuit interrupters are working by hitting the "test" button. If you stored your pump and filters for the winter, bring them out, reconnect them, and make sure they're in working order.

Clean out any pond debris that accumulated over the winter. Start biological filters once the water temperature remains above 50°F. When you put a biological filter back in service, it will take several weeks for the beneficial bacteria to reestablish a presence in the filter medium. You can buy starter bacteria from a water-garden supplier to speed up the colonization process.

As the weather warms, you may notice excessive algae (called an algal bloom). This problem will usually take care of itself once water lilies and other aquatic plants leaf out and begin providing shade and consuming nutrients.

Chemical Adjustments. Spring is a good time to check pH and water chemicals. If tests indicate that your water is polluted, you should replace a third of the water volume. Don't do this if the pond is undergoing an algae bloom, however, as that could make the problem worse. If you need to change the water, do it over a few days. If you add more than 5 percent of your pond's volume in a week, then dechlorinate the tap water.

Transplanting. Spring is the traditional time to add new plants to your water garden and to move or tidy up existing ones.

Fish Inspection. Fish are susceptible to stress after their winter fast. Give them a closer look if they show any signs of illness.

Oxygenated Water. Hotter weather means lower oxygen levels. To keep fish healthy, consider buying a kit to test for dissolved oxygen and an aerator to rescue fish in emergencies.

Late spring is the time to introduce new aquatic plants and to remove any dead foliage from existing ones. If you overwintered tropical water lilies, put the tubers in a shallow pan of water on a sunny windowsill about two months before the expected last frost in your area so that they can begin sprouting. Don't put them back in your pond before the water temperature reaches 70°F.

Divide water lilies, lotuses, and marginals with roots that are filling their pots. The best time to do this is after danger of frost has passed and before rapid growth resumes. Start giving lotuses fertilizer pellets twice a month; water lilies, once a month. Weed and mulch peripheral beds.

Frogs will begin singing and laying eggs. Fish, at first lethargic and weak from winter hibernation, will start to feed as the water temperature climbs toward 50°F. In the middle of the day, when their digestion is most active, offer them small amounts of high-carbohydrate foods containing wheat germ. Koi will like fresh salad greens.

Weather Changes. If the weather turns hot before water lilies have leafed out to provide shade, create temporary shade at one end of the pond with a tarp or other fabric held down with rocks. Because the fish have gone many weeks without food, they have a heightened susceptibility to stressors of all kinds. That means they're more likely to become ill, so check them frequently for unusual symptoms. Watch for blotchy or discolored skin, missing scales, or lethargic or erratic behavior. (See "Fish Diseases" on page 90.) If you treat your pond with a fungicide because your fish are ill, do so before starting a biological filter, because fungicides will also kill the beneficial bacteria that make the filter work. In mid- to late spring, you may see fish bumping and chasing each other because it's spawning time. To assist the process, you can buy spawning mats to place in the pond.

Summer

As the weather warms and fish become more active, you can give them high-protein foods such as chopped worms and daphnia (water fleas). In established and well-balanced ponds, they may get all the protein they need from insects and other small water creatures. Never overfeed fish: the rule of thumb is to give them no more food than they can eat within five minutes.

Oxygen. Because flora and fauna will be flourishing and multiplying, you should inspect the pump once a week and clean it as often as necessary. As the water heats, it's a good idea to run the pump continuously. Oxygen levels will drop, especially at night or during a thunderstorm. If you have fish, it's worth investing in a kit to test for dissolved oxygen. Blackened water, a foul smell, or fish gasping at the surface of the water is a sign that the oxygen level is dangerously low. For emergency aeration, you can spray the pond with a garden hose or use a separate aerator, which many pond owners find to be a worthwhile investment.

Spend a few minutes each day snipping off faded blossoms and keeping plants trimmed; such maintenance chores can be relaxing and give you additional quiet moments to enjoy your water garden. Insects will start to appear on plants, but avoid the use of insecticides in or near the pond. Handpick larger insects and dispose of them. Use a garden hose to spray aphids from water lilies, or wipe plant leaves with a damp cloth periodically. Once the water temperature reaches 75°F, step up fertilizing of water lilies to twice a month. Blanketweed, a filamentous alga, may be a problem in hot weather; if you twirl a long stick under it, it will wrap around the stick like cotton candy for easy removal. Add it, along with other skimmed materials and plant trimmings, to your compost heap.

Evaporation. As the weather becomes hotter, water evaporation will increase, so you'll need to top off the pond every day or two in order to keep the water level up. It's best to add a little water each day rather than a large amount once a week. Otherwise, if you use city-fed tap water, you'll need to dechlorinate it. You may find it helpful to store tap water in rain barrels, because chlorine will dissipate from the stored water. You can also set out plastic barrels to capture rainwater for topping off your pond. Remember to check it for pH, though, because rainwater can be highly acidic. Be vigilant about testing your pond's water quality at least once a month, or more frequently if you suspect a problem.

Autumn

Keep falling leaves from collecting in your pond or they'll decay and pollute the water. If the pond is under a tree, stretch netting over the pond and weigh it down with bricks or rocks. If leaves tend to blow into the pond from one direction, you may be able to keep them out with a line of netting or other temporary fencing. Scoop up floating leaves and other debris with a net. Remove any leaves that sink to the bottom of the pond with a soft plastic rake, pool sweep, or spa vacuum. (A pool sweep circulates water from your garden hose, so it may require you to dechlorinate your pond.)

Autumn is a good time to rein in rampantly growing

Handy Water Access. In summer, you'll need frequent access to water for aerating the pond, topping it off, and spraying pests off plants.

Leaf Shield. In autumn, installing a net over the pond will keep out falling leaves that can decay and pollute the water, which will cause more work next spring.

oxygenating plants, which should be thinned and cut back severely. Don't remove the turions, or overwintering buds, from plants such as frogbit. Cut back other aquatics as they go dormant; water lilies can be trimmed to about an inch above the container. Do not cut marginals below the water level. Remove tropical water lilies and other tender aquatics, and discard them or store them in their containers for the winter. If your pond has several depths, move water lilies to a level where the water will not freeze. If your pond might freeze below their crowns, you'll need to overwinter them in a frost-free place. Cattails and many of the ornamental grasses are beautiful in winter; don't cut them back until early spring.

Fish Food. As fish metabolism slows in preparation for winter, you should switch back to fish foods containing wheat germ. Gradually taper off the feedings to once every two to three days. Cease feeding as the fish become more lethargic and the water temperature drops to 50°F. When the water temperature drops below 45°F, fish become inactive and stop eating; you won't need to feed them again until the following spring. Refrain from feeding if fish become active during brief warm spells. In warmer climates (where water temperatures remain above 50°F), continue to feed fish all year, or as long as they remain active. As floating plants and water lilies die back, the fish will lose cover from predators, so lay down some sections

of 4-inch drainpipe where they can hide. (Black plastic is less visible than drain tiles, but it may need to be weighted down with a rock.)

A well-maintained pond won't need an annual stem-to-stern decontamination. But if yours is filled with grit and debris or tests show it to be polluted, autumn is the best time to drain and clean it. As days shorten and temperatures drop, most water plants are on their way to dormancy, and the increasingly drowsy fish are less likely to be stressed by a temporary relocation.

If you won't be running the pump during the winter, remove it from the pond, and clean all parts before storing it. Drain all pipes to keep them from cracking. Even if you'll be using your pump to keep the water from freezing as suggested on the next page, detach and clean fountain nozzles. External pumps should also be removed and tended. To avoid damage to a biological filter, drain, rinse, and store it.

Winter

If you live in a warm climate where freezes are rare, your pond duties won't change much in winter. Anywhere else, your main concern is to keep your pond from freezing for long periods. When ice forms on the pond, it can cut off oxygen to the fish and trap toxic gases beneath the surface. If the pond is frozen for more than a few days, fish may suffocate. (You should never break the ice, however, because the vibrations can injure your fish.) Ice can crack a concrete pond and may also damage inexpensive shells or the vertical sides of lined ponds.

Ice. Raised ponds are particularly susceptible to freezing. Plants and fish can't survive the winter in above-ground ponds except in frost-free areas. Protect a raised pond from ice damage in short freezes by covering it with boards and a tarp or similar heavy material. You can also keep ice from exerting pressure on the sides of the pond by floating something in it—rubber balls, wooden planks, a couple of milk jugs. This will work for in-ground ponds, too, where freezes are infrequent or of short duration.

In mild climates, where ice is a temporary condition, you can place a pot of boiling water on top of the ice to melt a hole in it. Use a pot with a hole in the handle, and run a heavy string through the hole. You can then retrieve the pot if it melts through the ice and falls to the bottom of the pond.

Winter Care. Many types of fish can spend winter in your pond as long as the surface doesn't freeze solid. Ice cuts off their oxygen and traps toxic gases. A pond deicer is the most reliable solution.

In moderately cold climates, raise a circulating pump off the pond bottom (so it doesn't circulate cold water into the bottom where fish and plants are keeping warm), and direct the outward flow up with a short tube or pipe; this will keep ice from forming in that part of the pond. The easiest way to keep a pond ice-free, and the only way in extremely cold climates, is to buy a floating pond deicer to keep a hole open in the ice all winter. These devices are controlled by a thermostat, so they run only when needed, and (of course) should be plugged into a circuit with a ground-fault interrupter. Keep snow off the ice surface so that light reaches the bottom of the pond.

Planning. Use winter downtime to your advantage. Make observations about your pond's microclimates, and consider planting shrubs to block stiff cold winds, or figure out where to move slow-growing water lilies so they get more sun. Winter is the traditional time to order plants for the coming spring. Also replenish your supply of snails or tadpoles, if necessary, and any testing kits or plumbing supplies you expect to need. Suppliers will wait to ship plants and animals until it's safe to put them outside in your area.

Troubleshooting

Your ability to observe and respond to small changes in the pond environment—whether it's a different color to the water, altered behavior in your fish, or a slight shift in your edging—can save you more expense and heartache down the line. The solution to serious problems may involve emptying the pond of water and quickly refilling it with the least amount of trauma to its inhabitants.

Maintaining the Pond

A well-maintained pond should only need cleaning every three or four years. You should avoid cleaning wildlife ponds if possible, because the microorganisms and small creatures in the water are all important to the ecosystem you want to maintain. It can take many months to reestablish a good balance.

But if the water is choked with algae, filled with sediment, or severely polluted, you may have to completely drain the pond, scrub it down, and refill it with fresh water. Draining may also be necessary to find and repair a leak in the pond liner or shell. (See "Repairing a Pond Foundation," page 84.) The best time to clean the pond is in late summer or early autumn. If you clean the pond in the spring, you might disrupt spawning fish and amphibians or destroy the eggs, or damage emerging plant shoots. And cleaning a pond in midsummer is like trying to make a bed with people still lying in it; it's much harder, plus it upsets the sleepers!

The best time to divide water plants and marginals is after danger of frost has passed, above. If you live in a warm climate where freezes are rare, your pond duties won't change much in winter, below.

Draining and Cleaning the Pond

1 Drain the Pond. Arrange the pond cleaning for a time when you can drain and refill the pond as quickly as possible. You don't want to leave a flexible liner exposed, or aquatic plants out of the water, any longer than absolutely necessary.

Before you start, prepare one or more holding tubs for your fish. You'll need about a gallon of water for each inch of fish (i.e., one 5-inch fish in a 5-gallon bucket). If you have a lot of fish, a children's plastic wading pool or 50-gallon plastic trash can works well. Place either in the shade; fill with some of the pond water; and add a few bunches of oxygenating plants to the tank.

Drain the pond to about 6 inches above the bottom; then carefully net out the fish and put them in the holding tub. If the fish will be out of the pond for more than a few hours, place an aquarium air bubbler in the tank to provide additional oxygen. If your property slopes and your pond is situated slightly uphill, you can use a garden hose to simply siphon out the water to a lower area of your yard. Otherwise, you can use your pond's pump to pump the water out.

Tools & Materials

- Holding tub (plastic wading pool or trash can)
- Plastic buckets; fish net
- Newspaper or burlap (for water plants)
- Plastic dustpan
- Aquarium air bubbler (for lengthy cleaning/repairs)
- Garden hose and adapter for pond pump (if available), or sump pump
- Soft-bristled brush (optional)
- Water purifier or dechlorinating agent; thermometer

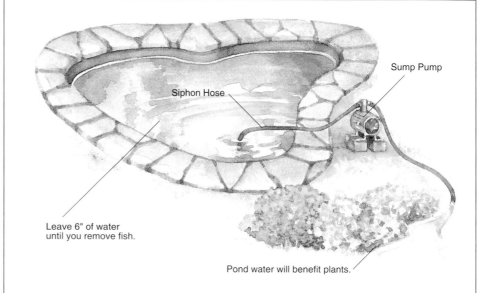

Siphon Hose
Sump Pump
Leave 6" of water until you remove fish.
Pond water will benefit plants.

1 Remove the water to about 6 in. deep. Use a siphon hose, the pond pump, or a high-capacity sump pump to drain the pond.

SMART TIP

Some common pond problems include water that stays green into summer. Correct the problem by remove debris from the bottom and adding more oxygenating and floating plants. If your fish appear to be gasping for air at the surface, add oxygen to the water through a garden hose or aerator. If the water level drops after you top off the pond, suspect a leak in the liner. For water that turns black and smells unpleasant, aerate with a garden hose and add submerged plants.

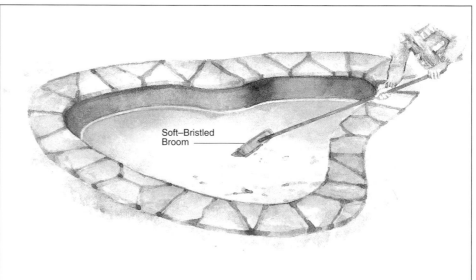

Soft–Bristled Broom

3 Clean pond gently. Use soft tools that won't damage your liner or shell.

Garden hose adapters are available for many pond pumps. If you can't get an adapter for your particular pump or you can't use the pump to remove the water for some other reason (because it's a slow process and you simply can't spare that much time), you can rent a high-capacity sump pump at most tool rental shops or home centers.

Run the pumped out water into a nearby garden area; the nutrients it contains will benefit your plants. Don't allow the pump to run dry, or the motor will burn out. At this point, you will be glad if you have followed the advice to create a sump area when building your pond. (See page 24.) It will ensure that your motor does not run dry before you have most of your water pumped out and will leave you a smaller area of water and muck to bail out by hand. To avoid damaging your liner or shell, always use a plastic bucket to bail out any remaining water.

2 Remove the Wildlife. You'll have to take measures to preserve the fish and plants. All of your oxygenating plants will have to be submerged in holding tanks or buckets; it's often easiest to make new bunches of stems and repot them in fresh soil. Water lilies and marginals need to be kept moist and out of the wind. Wrap them in wet newspapers or burlap sacks; put them in a shady location; and spray them occasionally with a garden hose.

When the pond is drained, sift through the silt, and pick out as many snails as you can find. (You probably won't get them all.) Put these snails in the holding tank with the fish. Use a plastic dustpan to shovel out the silt on the pond bottom.

3 Clean the Pond. Carefully scrub the sides and bottom with a soft-bristled brush or a strong jet of water from a garden hose; don't use chemical cleaners, and be careful not to tear or puncture the liner or pond shell. Rinse and drain the pond several times in order to remove any remaining muck. Once the liner is completely clean, inspect it carefully for leaks. This is a good time to make liner repairs.

4 Add Fresh Water. Refill the pond with fresh water. Unless you are using well water, add a dechlorinating agent or water purifier. Pour a few buckets of the original pond water back into the pond to help establish the biological balance. Reintroduce your plants now, but don't put the fish back into the pond until the water temperature returns to within 5 degrees of the temperature in the holding tank. Don't forget: as with new ponds, you can expect increased growth of algae until the ecological balance is reestablished.

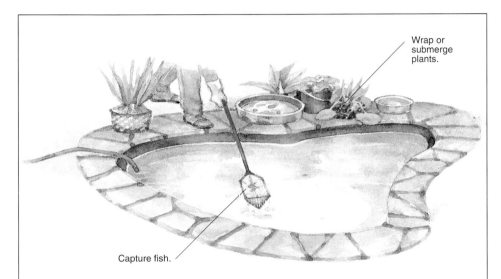

Wrap or submerge plants.

Capture fish.

2 Preserve fish and plants. Place fish, snails, and other pond life in tubs filled with pond water. Aerate the water if necessary. Submerge or wet-wrap plants as appropriate. Finish emptying the pond.

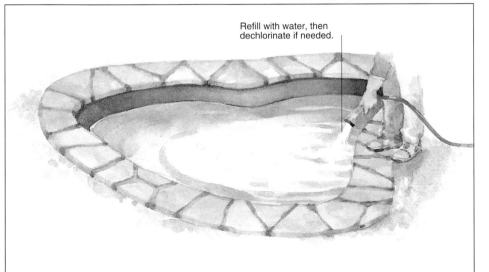

Refill with water, then dechlorinate if needed.

4 Refill pond. Treat any water imbalances; reintroduce plants; then add fish when water warms.

Repairing a Pond Foundation

If you were careful when installing the liner or shell, didn't add a 200-pound statue without a footing, and avoided wading across the pond in your golf cleats, the chances are good that your foundation will meet or exceed its life expectancy. But accidents happen to even the most careful pond keepers: big branches fall, big dogs drop by for an uninvited romp, big rocks tumble from the edging. Here's what to do if your pond is leaking.

Flexible Liners. If flexible liners develop punctures or tears before the end of their life expectancy, it's worth repairing them with patching kits available from water-garden dealers. The kits usually contain a small can of adhesive and a piece of liner for making patches; some come with double-sided tape rather than adhesive.

1 Locate the Source of the Leak. Eliminate a waterfall as the source of the leak by shutting it off, topping off the pond, and seeing if the level still goes down. If not, the leak is somewhere along the sides of your waterfall or in the tubing between your pump and outlet. If you still don't find it, check all around the pond's edges to make sure a spot hasn't settled lower than the water level. Eventually the water will stop leaking at the level of the leak. Add water to just above this level. Then add some milk or food coloring around the edges of the pond; either will dissipate everywhere else but form a direct line toward a leak. Drain the pond to below the leak. (You'll have to remove fish and plants if it's near the bottom of the pond.) If it appears that the leak was caused by a rock or root under the liner, remove the offending object. Cushion the area behind the tear with damp sand or a piece of liner underlayment.

2 Wipe off the Leak Area. Make sure the tear or puncture is completely clean and dry. This is important because otherwise the adhesive you will be using on the liner material and the patch will not adhere properly.

3 Brush on Adhesive. Cut a patch from the same material as the liner (PVC plastic or rubber) that is about 2 inches wider and longer than the tear. Apply a thin, even coat of adhesive over and slightly beyond the torn area.

4 Coat the Patch. Apply a coat of adhesive to the back of the patch, making sure you cover it completely. Allow the adhesive to become slightly tacky (about 2 to 3 minutes, or as recommended on the label directions).

5 Adhere the Patch. Firmly press the patch down, and smooth it to remove wrinkles. If possible, weight the patch with a bag of sand. Allow the adhesive to dry thoroughly before filling the pond.

Rigid Ponds. Leaks in rigid pond shells are rare. They usually indicate an uneven base (in which case you will find the leak along the rim) or a sharp stone under the shell (you'll find a leak farther down). You can repair the leak with a fiberglass boat repair kit, which includes a resin and a catalyst that need to be mixed as an adhesive, along with a fiberglass mesh patch.

After locating the leak, drain the pond and either level the shell bottom or look for and remove any object that may have caused the puncture. You can patch the shell before or after returning it to the hole, whichever seems easier. With sandpaper, roughen the area around the leak so the patch will stick. Mix the resin and catalyst, spread the adhesive on the patch, and apply the patch to the leak. Follow directions for drying before refilling the pond.

Concrete Ponds. Concrete ponds crack easily when improperly installed. You may be able to patch one or two small cracks with a caulk and neoprene rubber coating sold for this purpose. Or you can try to rescue a pond by installing a flexible liner on top of the concrete. Sand down rough spots; fill deep crevices; and install an underlayment before lining.

Tools & Materials

- Scissors or utility knife
- Milk or food coloring
- Buckets (for fish)
- Wet newspaper (for wrapping plants)
- Sand
- Liner underlayment
- Cloth
- Utility paint brush
- Liner patch material
- Liner adhesive
- Weight (sandbag, etc.)

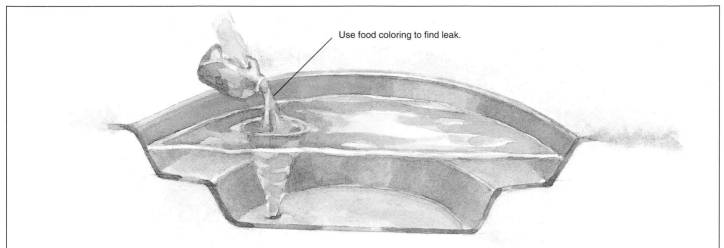

Use food coloring to find leak.

1 Pour some milk or food coloring around the edges of the pond; either will dissipate everywhere else but form a direct line toward a leak.

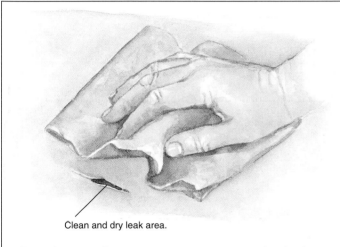

Clean and dry leak area.

2 Make sure the tear or puncture is completely clean and dry.

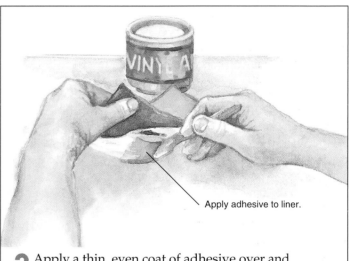

Apply adhesive to liner.

3 Apply a thin, even coat of adhesive over and slightly beyond the torn area.

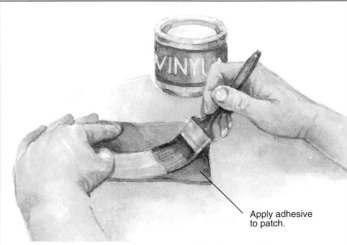

Apply adhesive to patch.

4 Apply a coat of adhesive to the back of the patch, making sure you cover it completely.

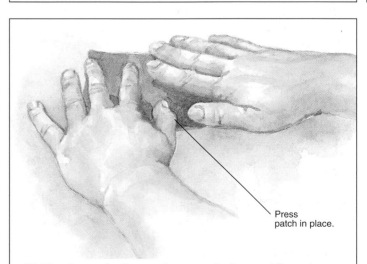

Press patch in place.

5 Firmly apply the patch; smooth down. Allow the adhesive to dry thoroughly before filling the pond.

adding fish

FISH AND OTHER AQUATIC LIFE bring a whole new level of vibrancy to a garden pond. They are fun to watch, and they contribute to the pond's ecosystem. But to keep them happy and healthy, there are steps you must take to improve water quality so that the fish you select for your pond adapt and thrive in their new environment.

Fish

Doctors, dentists, and psychologists often have aquariums in their waiting rooms. They know that the sight of fish swimming to-and-fro is almost hypnotic, making us feel more relaxed and peaceful. Fish have the same calming effect in an outdoor pond, whether they're rare, 2-foot-long koi or a school of common minnows. Add to that the fun of seeing them race to gobble a handful of food or chase each other as frenetically as Harpo Marx during their annual mating ritual, and fish seem as indispensable to a pond as water lilies. In addition to being captivating, fish will help control bugs, provide nutrients for plants, and keep plants from spreading too fast. They are an integral part of a pond's thriving ecosystem.

Keep in mind, though, that adding fish to your pond also adds new challenges. Fish can eat prized plants, add waste that clouds the water, and break your heart by becoming dinner for any number of potential predators. You need to decide before you build your pond whether you want large fish such as koi, which need both ample room to swim around and extra depth for hiding and for surviving winter. Other fish likewise benefit from a deeper pond area, which will stay cooler and retain more oxygen in hot weather. Unlike water lilies, many fish will be better off in a shady pond. If your pond isn't in partial shade, you will need to create shade by introducing enough floating or floating-leaved plants, such as water lilies, to cover roughly half the pond's surface.

Predators can find your fish even if you have a formal pool on an urban patio; you'll need to create hiding places for fish with overhangs along the edge, terra-cotta drainage tiles, or black-plastic drainpipes weighted down on the pond bottom. You can create additional hideaways by the way you arrange your plants: fish can take refuge among the stems of oxygenators and marginals or under floating leaves. Without water plants, you'll have additional concerns besides creating hiding places. You will need to feed your fish more often and invest in a good artificial filter to remove fish waste.

You'll minimize catastrophes and maximize enjoyment if you study this chapter and learn the needs of fish before you buy them. Fish, like pets, plants, and other living things, can get sick and die without proper care. While you don't have to take fish for walks, remember that they are outdoor pets in an environment that will never be completely natural. Plan ahead to make that environment as healthy for them as possible.

Containing Pond Creatures

Never dispose of your fish, snails, or other pond life in nearby waterways or sewers. Animals outside their natural environments, just like non-native plants, can upset the healthy balance of waterways. (See "Beware of Invasive Plants" on page 96 for a discussion of troublesome plant species.) Water creatures that have caused the most trouble have been introduced by commerce: zebra mussel in ships' ballasts, tilapia to raise for food markets, trout for sport. The bullfrog has been taken beyond its native range in the eastern and central United States by connoisseurs of frog's legs, and in their new homes these amphibians are wiping out small native frogs. These animals don't just dominate native species by eating them or their food; they can also spread diseases for which native animals have no resistance. For example, the common carp—a relative of koi—carries some 130 different parasites.

Home Sweet Home. Keeping a few fish of any kind are reason enough to create a water garden. If you decide to incorporate fish into your plans, make a commitment to monitor their environment in order to keep them healthy.

To keep fish healthy, pond water needs to stay within certain parameters. These include moderate temperatures, a sufficient oxygen content, a relatively neutral pH (a measure of the water's acidity/alkalinity), the absence of chlorine compounds, and minimal amounts of nitrites and ammonia (which come from both fish waste and fertilizer runoff).

Some chemicals used to purify water are toxic to fish. If your water comes from municipal or county sources, you'll need to check with local authorities to determine what chemicals are used to purify the water supply. If your water contains only ordinary chlorine, uncompounded with other chemicals, the chlorine will dissipate within 24 to 48 hours after you fill the pond. If your water supply contains chloramine (a

A Healthy Environment. Just because your pond water is clear doesn't necessarily mean it's healthy for fish. Regular monitoring of water quality will prevent problems.

compound of chlorine and ammonia) or chlorine dioxide, you'll need to treat the water with a dechlorinating agent, available from water-garden suppliers. Even if your water is free of these substances, it's a good idea to delay introducing fish until the plants have had a couple of weeks to become established, algae has cleared, and the pond's normal population of beneficial microscopic creatures has built up.

To monitor the water-quality parameters most important for fish, you will probably want the following items.

■ **A thermometer.** This is not so important for goldfish, which can tolerate a broad range of temperatures, but it is crucial for some other fish that can't survive water temperatures above 70°F.

■ **A kit for testing pH.** Fish need a pH level near neutral, (between 6.6 and 7.5). You should test your water supply to see whether it falls within this range; test the pond again after it's filled with plants and animals. Retest the water periodically to make sure the pH stays within the recommended range, especially after adding more than 20 percent new water or after introducing new fish and plants.

Water from some wells is naturally alkaline; if your water is hard, it will probably be alkaline too. (Both calcium and magnesium, often the cause of hard water, also cause alkalinity.) If you use a water softener or a water conditioner, don't use the treated water for your

fish—or plants. If you don't already have a direct line for outdoor or garden use, install an outdoor faucet that connects directly to the water supply and bypasses the water conditioner or softener.

Water can become alkaline if your pool is concrete, from contact with mortared edges, or if you use concrete blocks to raise water plants. Algae can sometimes change the pH level. You may also want to have on hand products for adjusting pH.

■ **A kit for testing ammonia and/or nitrites.** Some water-testing kits will also test for ammonia and nitrites, which can build up from fish waste when a pond is overpopulated. If your test kit doesn't, you'll need to buy a separate testing kit.

■ **Dechlorinating formula.** This is essential if your water supply contains chloramine or chlorine dioxide. You'll especially need it during the summer, when it's important to keep ponds topped off with water. You can safely add up to 5 percent of pond volume once or twice a week without using a dechlorinator; if you add more, you'll need to retreat the water. Adding water with a spray or sprinkler will help dissipate ordinary chlorine as well as add some oxygen.

■ **Rock salt or pond salt.** Fish have a coating of mucus that protects them from disease but that can be lost when they are stressed. Periodic treatment of the pond with rock salt (not iodized table salt) at the rate of 2 pounds per 100 gallons will restore this protection. Salt corrects the electrolyte balance of the fish and helps prevent the loss of fluids. Salt manufactured especially for ponds includes beneficial trace elements. It's not good for plants, though, so it should be added to the pond as far away from plants as possible. If you prefer not to add salt to the pond water, you can give fish a salt bath. (See the aquarium discussion below.)

■ **A parasite treatment or preventive.** Use this when you add new fish—especially if they haven't been treated by the dealer—or when you spot the symptoms of parasites. (See "Fish Diseases" on page 91 for a discussion of various parasites.)

■ **An aeration kit.** The oxygen content of your pond can decrease rapidly in thunderstorms or during a sudden change in air temperature. (Warm water doesn't hold oxygen as well as cooler water does.) This kit may be needed to restore the oxygen level for your fish. Also, fish may suffer from an oxygen deficit at night, when plants release carbon dioxide, so it's usually a good idea to leave your waterfall, fountain, or other aeration device operating all night. (You can also help aerate the pond by splashing water in with a hose or even by stirring it.)

■ **One or more plastic buckets for transporting fish.** For medium-size fish, a 5-gallon bucket is a good size; for large fish, get a short, wide bucket.

■ **A soft net (on a pole) for guiding fish into the bucket.** Lifting fish out of the water in a net is stressful to them, so you should use the net only to steer them into the bucket.

■ **An aquarium.** You'll need to use an aquarium as a "hospital tank" for treating sick fish, as a holding tank to inspect new fish before adding them to your pond, or as a winter home for the fish if you live in a cold climate. Consult an aquarium dealer about what size to buy. Obviously, size isn't as important if one or two fish will be in the tank for a few hours as it will be if you bring all your pond residents indoors for several months.

The aquarium should be filled with water from the pond, unless you have reason to believe something is wrong with the water quality. It should be connected to an aeration device of some kind, as sick fish will be additionally stressed by a lack of oxygen. Medications in the water also increase the need for aeration. Keep the tank out of direct sun for extended periods so that the water doesn't heat up too much for the fish.

If you don't want to add rock salt to your pond as discussed above, use the aquarium for a salt bath, and then return the treated fish to your pond.

Bringing Fish Home

Don't buy your fish until the water temperature in your pond consistently stays at least 50°F, which is the temperature at which most species become active in spring. If you have a reputable pond supplier in your area, it's worth driving out of your way to buy fish there. The salespeople will be more knowledgeable; they will probably offer a guarantee; and when they slip your new fish in a plastic bag for the ride home, they will inject the bag with oxygen.

Certain mail-order water-garden suppliers ship fish over long distances, although spending a day or two in the belly of a plane at a variety of different temperatures will stress out even the most well-packaged creature.

Fish from a pet store may have a harder time making the transition from indoors to out. But if buying fish this way seems your only option, study the list of fish diseases on page 91 so that you can identify a sickly fish. Ask the store staff whether they guarantee the fish's health for a length of time, and if they can treat the fish for parasites before you take them home. On the ride home, keep the fish in a cool, dark place. A picnic cooler with a lid is a handy way to transport them. Don't put them in the trunk or keep them in a closed car while you run other errands.

Lower the bag into the pond, and add some of the pond water. Doing this over a period of 10 to 15 minutes will ease the transition to a different temperature and different water quality. It's best not to add the water from the bag to the pond, on the chance that it contains parasites. Instead, ease the fish out with your hand or, less desirably, a net.

Watch the fish for an hour. Fish may try to jump out of a new pond. If they continue to jump out or gasp, check the water. Move them to an aquarium to fix the problem. Feed the fish sparingly for the next couple of days.

Careful Handling. When bringing new fish home or when moving them around, handle with care. They are easily stressed and do better with a gradual transition.

Feeding Your Fish

In a well-balanced pond, fish theoretically do not need to be fed at all. But supplemental feeding is usually necessary. Besides, you'll enjoy watching them scurry after their food and hurry to the water's edge to greet you.

Fish need supplemental food in spring and fall. They become active as soon as the water has reached 50°F in spring, but this early in the season not many plants will have leafed out yet, nor will there be many insects and other little creatures for them to feast on. At this time, don't feed your fish protein. Instead, choose wheat germ or similar high-carbohydrate foods, which are easy for fish to digest. Once the water has warmed another 10°F or so and their activity level rises dramatically, they will need more protein in the form of chopped worms, daphnia (also called water fleas), or some frozen or freeze-dried fish foods. (Daphnia can be seen as pale pink clouds in the water and will help keep the pond clean by eating free floating algae.) Most fish-food products on the market contain around 40 percent protein, which should be adequate in a balanced pond.

These supplements come in sticks, pellets, or flakes. All of these forms float, which allows you to net out un-eaten food and keep the pond clean. A granular form, although often less expensive, will sink; you'll save money, but you can't be sure how much is turning into waste at the bottom of your pond. This waste is a potential cause of disease, so definitely avoid overfeeding your fish.

Feeding Schedule. Feed your fish once or twice each day when spring first arrives; then gradually decrease your feedings to every other day or so. They should survive quite well without feeding if you take a short vacation. Never feed them more food than they can eat in five minutes, and use a net to remove any food that remains. Avoid feeding them late in the day. Their metabolism goes up after they eat, so they then need more oxygen; because plants give off carbon dioxide at night, less oxygen will be available to the fish then. Cut back gradually on food as temperatures drop in autumn and fish become less active. Stop feeding for the winter once water temperatures fall below 50°F. Your fish will survive the winter by living off the fat they have stored. They will use these resources slowly because their metabolism has slowed.

Sometimes diseased fish will benefit from a change of diet; try a different brand of fish food, and see whether your fish improve. Members of the carp family will also eat worms as well as vegetables that humans eat, such as lettuce scraps and peas.

Spawning

Fish play their mating game in late spring and early summer, usually when the water has warmed to between 54° and 60°F. Males get tiny white bumps on their gills and some become brighter colored. Females take on a slightly pregnant look because their ovaries are bulging with thousands of eggs.

A frantic morning chase around the pond convinces the female to lay her eggs, usually on an underwater plant, after which the male fertilizes them with his sperm, or milt. Babies, known as fry, hatch about a week later and spend the first day clinging to the plant or the side of the pond or hanging vertically in the water, absorbing their egg sacs for nutrition.

Fish fry are vulnerable not only to pond insects and other predators too small to bother adult fish but also to other fish species and even to their own parents. If you want to save as many fry as possible, buy a spawning mat (not unlike a crude welcome mat) to put on the pond bottom. Remove it to an aquarium when you see eggs on its surface. The young fry need a high-protein diet of flakes, brine shrimp, or daphnia.

Serene Setting. Fish and other creatures bring new dimensions of movement and color to your water garden.

Ecologically Balanced Home. A well-balanced pond is a healthy home for fish, but you'll still have to feed them.

Fish Diseases

Even a novice can spot many of the changes in behavior or appearance that mean a fish is ill. A sick fish may act lethargic or huddle against the edge of the pond, gasp for air, swim frantically and bump the pond edge, or be bullied by other fish. It might clamp its fins against its body or develop red veins or fins, or its dorsal (spine) fin may droop.

If you see unusual symptoms, check the water temperature, pH, and levels of ammonia and nitrites to determine whether any of these is stressing the fish.

If fish are clearly ill, it's often best to remove them to an aquarium, where you can treat them with a medicine or salt bath and keep the disease from spreading to the rest of the pond inhabitants. Handle the fish as little as possible to minimize additional stress. Net each fish underwater, guide it into an underwater bowl or bucket, and then lift out the bowl and lower it into the aquarium water.

Some of the more common fish diseases are described below. Consult your supplier or a veterinarian for more specific treatments.

■ **Anchor Worm.** This isn't a disease but a tubelike parasite, about ¾ inch long, which attaches under the fish's gill with its hooked head while it produces two eggs at its nether end. The main symptom is a swelling where the parasite is attached. Catch the fish, and remove each anchor worm with tweezers; then treat the spot with an antiseptic such as merbromin or iodine (from a drugstore).

■ **Dropsy.** This ailment, most often caused by bacteria, has such a telltale symptom that it's sometimes called the pinecone disease: the fish swells, and its scales bristle away from its sides, making it look like a pinecone. Fish will also get bug-eyed. A salt-bath treatment may help.

■ **Finrot, or Bodyrot.** The fish—often a fantail or a shubunkin—develops a white line on its caudal area (where the body joins the tail), and this area becomes inflamed. The tissue disintegrates and needs to be gently removed with a sharp knife; then the fish is put on treatment with a special antibiotic. It's always an excellent idea to consult a veterinarian before you administer antibiotics, just to make certain that you're using the correct medication and dosage.

■ **Flukes.** There are both gill and skin flukes; in either case they are microscopic, parasitic flatworms. When they prey on fish, you'll see excess mucus plus irritated puffy patches or loss of color, and the fish will act irritated, banging against objects, twitching their fins, and opening and closing their mouths rapidly. A salt bath may help remove the flukes.

■ **Fungus.** When fish are stressed and their protective mucous layer breaks down, they become susceptible to fungi normally present in pond water. Instead of tolerating these fungi, the fish sprout cottony growths. Most fish suppliers sell fungicides that can treat the problem.

■ **Lice.** These flat, gelatinous creatures are only ¼ inch long but have clearly visible legs and eyespots. The tissue damage they cause by attaching themselves to the fish, often on the fins and gills, can eventually prove fatal to the victim. Remove lice deftly with tweezers, and treat the fish with an antiseptic such as iodine.

■ **Tuberculosis.** This is a highly contagious bacterial disease that can cause rapid weight loss, as the human version does. Fish may lose color and develop raw swollen patches, and fins may waste away. It is almost always fatal. Remove any fish from the pond as soon as you suspect it is tubercular.

■ **Ulcers.** Bacteria common to pond water will cause stressed fish to develop ulcers, popped eyes, bloody patches, and ragged-looking fins. Treat with an antibiotic.

■ **White Spot.** Fish with this disease (technically, ichthyophthiriasis, or "ich" for short) will have spots like grains of salt all over its body, and because they itch, the fish may bump against the sides of the pond. White spot is caused by the parasitic protozoan *Ichthyophthirius multifilis*. Consult your dealer or veterinarian about a cure.

Keeping Healthy Fish

- Test water quality regularly. If you have a lot of fish, be particularly vigilant about ammonia and nitrite levels.
- Be prepared to remove fish quickly. Have an aquarium or other hospital tank available should they display any signs of distress or illness.
- Be aware of predators. Install protective netting or fencing if you see birds or animals lurking around your pond.
- Find a reliable expert. Have a contact number handy for a trusted supplier or veterinarian whom you can call for advice.

Choosing Your Fish

If you have an existing pond, you will have to select the species and number of fish appropriate to its conditions. If you're still in the planning stages, check the entries in this section to see which varieties of fish are most adaptable to your needs. A common rule for stocking your pond is that 1 square foot of well-balanced pond water can support 2 inches of fish. Koi are an exception to this rule; they require 25 square feet each.

In addition to the size of your pond, there are other factors to consider. Tropical fish species will need to be removed each fall and kept in an indoor aquarium. Other species are very sensitive to high temperatures and will get sluggish or even die during hot summers.

If you want to create a wildlife pond, you may want to focus on native fish. Expect a natural pond to attract fish-eating birds and raccoons.

Comet. There are several strains of comet, but all of them can tolerate both hot and cold temperature extremes.

Common Goldfish. Both colorful and tough, the common goldfish, a popular indoor pet, is also a good candidate for your pond.

Shubunkin. A goldfish relative, Shubunkin come in a multitude of colors, including blues and purples.

Fantail. Long fins and tail give Fantail a ballroom dancer's appearance. It's not as hardy, though, as some other goldfish.

Moor. The better to see you with, say the comical popping eyes of this fantail strain called Moor. The dark body can be difficult to spot.

Koi. Members of the carp family, Koi need room—25 square feet per fish. Some of the elaborately patterned specimens are costly.

Rudd. Although it is a compact species, the rudd needs a spacious pond as well as a lot of submerged plants to encourage breeding.

Butterfly Koi. If you don't have a big enough pond for other koi, try this small type called Butterfly, which is surprisingly hardy.

Tench. A school of tench is like having a professional sanitation crew at work. They're always cleaning the bottom of the pond.

Orfe. These frisky schooling fish will entertain you by leaping from the pond for insects. It can grow up to 18 inches long.

Mosquito Fish. Even the smallest pond can use a population of Mosquito Fish to gobble the larvae of mosquitos and midges.

9 Adding Fish

chapter 10
adding plants

NOW YOU'RE READY TO CHOOSE PLANTS for your water garden. There are absolutely no limits to your choices. In fact, you can decide not to have any plants at all! For example, a small, formal pool set into a stone patio is not a place where most plants will thrive—such a design is often just about water. But from this extreme, there is a spectrum of landscaping possibilities.

Any pond with some area of still water can be home to a few water lilies or an elegant lotus. Most water gardeners will grow underwater plants because of the important biological functions they perform. On the margins of your pond, you can plant a single clump of exquisite Japanese irises or a vast collection of wetland plants and cattails. If you grow roses in another area of your garden, a formal pool surrounded by rose topiaries might be wholly appropriate. On a sweeping lawn, you might choose a slightly less formal water feature with a single dramatic clump of ornamental grasses or a huge swath of them—depending on the size of both the yard and the pond.

Choosing Plants

Look for plants that blend with the design of your water feature and the rest of your yard. Whether your design is formal or informal will affect the way you use plants. Formal gardens employ plants in ways that make human intervention obvious—they are probably carefully pruned and trained in geometric beds or in planters. To complement a formal pool, limit your choices to a few plants. You can choose a single dramatic specimen—a solitary bonsai on a pedestal or a weeping cherry tree. An informal pond calls for a planting area with sweeping curves and

a relaxed mix of plants in a variety of shapes, textures, and colors.

There are a number of practical uses for plants around your water garden: for reducing wind, discouraging predators, framing views, and defining paths. And you'll certainly want to take advantage of your pond's ability to reflect plants with colorful foliage and dramatic shapes, and to situate fragrant plants near benches or other stopping places.

To make your water garden an integral part of your landscape, you may want to choose flowers with colors that echo those elsewhere in your garden. Light affects how we see color. In a bright, sunny garden, hot colors such as reds, oranges, and bright yellows stand out. If your garden is somewhat shady, or if you're designing an evening garden (one you won't usually visit until the sun is low), cool blues, pinks, and especially whites will seem to glow in the fading light and create a tranquil atmosphere.

Still, many people focus too much on the color of flowers. Most plants won't bloom all season (except for annuals), so try to include plants with attractive foliage to provide interest when the flowers have faded. Foliage can serve as more than a backdrop to flowers; you can design a gorgeous all-season display by featuring plants that are handsome primarily for the color, shape, and texture of their leaves. Water-lily leaves have interesting patterns that change daily; those of lotuses are fluted and waxy so they capture raindrops. Leaves of floating plants can look like lettuce, clovers, or green snowflakes.

Around your pond, go for variety: big bold leaves, such as those of ligularia; vertical leaves, such as those of irises and grasses; lacy and delicate ferns; and creeping plants that will spread and even drape over the edge of

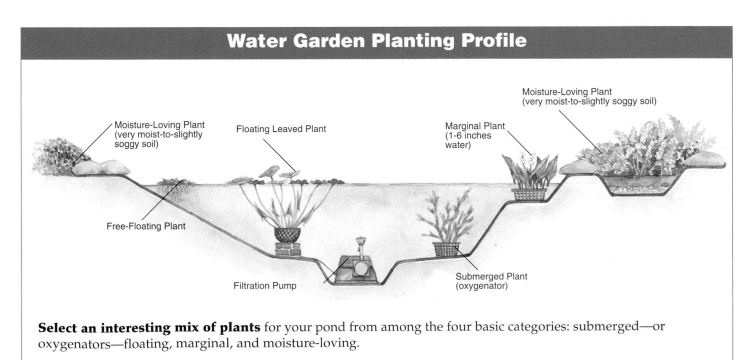

Water Garden Planting Profile

Moisture-Loving Plant
(very moist-to-slightly soggy soil)

Moisture-Loving Plant
(very moist-to-slightly soggy soil)

Floating Leaved Plant

Marginal Plant
(1-6 inches water)

Free-Floating Plant

Filtration Pump

Submerged Plant
(oxygenator)

Select an interesting mix of plants for your pond from among the four basic categories: submerged—or oxygenators—floating, marginal, and moisture-loving.

your pond to help hide its edge. Avoid going overboard by trying to plant one of everything, though. Repeating one or two plants—or echoing one or two colors, textures, or shapes—will make a variety of plants look like a coherent design.

No garden is ever finished. Some plants may die, and others may simply fail to satisfy. But if you're like most people who enjoy gardening, every year will bring the discovery of new varieties that you will want to try. Approach your garden design as an adventure—an exciting exploration of the vast world of plants.

The Roles Plants Play

Most water gardeners will choose at least some traditional water-garden plants, which fall into the four categories described below.

■ **Submerged plants** are those that grow below the water surface. Also called oxygenators, these plants act as natural filters to help keep your pond in chemical and biological balance, making it more hospitable for fish and less inviting to algae. In fact, submerged plants are a necessity if you want fish and aren't going to invest in a biological filter.

■ **Floating plants** either float freely on the surface of the pond or are rooted in containers on the bottom and send up leaves that float. They help to discourage the formation of algae by keeping the water cool and shady. Floaters include lotuses and water lilies, which many people consider a must for a pond.

■ **Marginal plants** are those that like to grow in very shallow water or at the mucky edge (margin) of a pond or lake. You can grow most of them right in your pond if you plant them in containers raised on shelves or blocks to their preferred level. Plants in this category are especially useful for creating the look of a natural pond and help conceal the edge of a flexible liner or rigid shell.

■ **Moisture-loving and bog plants** make up a broad category that includes almost any plant that likes very moist to slightly soggy soil (more moisture than is found in the average garden, but not standing water). In a natural environment, a lake, pond, or stream will be surrounded by a transitional zone of relatively wet soil that supports a fascinating array of plants. Include some of these plants if you want to create as natural-looking a pond as possible.

Even when surrounding a less "wild" pond, some of these plants—willows, irises, and ornamental grasses, for example—simply look right near a bog pond. So don't be afraid to include them in the overall design. True bog plants are a subcategory of moisture lovers. These species require a more specialized environment of very acid soil and low oxygen.

Beware of Invasive Plants

A number of plants that are still sold for water gardens are invasive, meaning that they will take over any area where they grow, dimishing niches for other plants and disrupting the natural food chain. Even if you think you can contain them in an enclosed water garden, the danger of their escaping through seeds carried by wind, birds, or insects is real. If you never plant any of these invasives, you'll never have to worry about them.

Because invasives vary by region, it's best to contact your local chapter of The Nature Conservancy or your Cooperative Extension Office to learn which plants to avoid. The plants on this page are well-known pests in large areas of North America, so unless you know that they aren't invasive in your area, don't plant them.

Eichhornia Crassipes Water hyacinth

Myriophyllum Spicatum Eurasian watermilfoil

Phragmites Australis Common reed

Melaleuca Quinquenervia Punk tree or Paperbark Tea tree

Iris Pseudacorus Yellow flag iris

Lythrum Salicaria Purple loosestrife

Hydrilla Verticillata Hydrilla

Tamarix Species Tamarix

Submerged plants, or oxygenators, are the lungs and kidneys of a water garden. During the day, they produce oxygen that helps support fish and other pond animals, and they also filter mineral salts and fish wastes that would otherwise promote the growth of algae and/or build to damaging levels. A few of these plants offer a visual bonus: they produce flowers above the waterline. Many others resemble a bird's plumage.

Plant oxygenators in your pond a few weeks before introducing fish to allow them to become established and also so they can begin filtering the water. Plant them in sand or gravel, not soil, or simply weight them in groups on the pond bottom. In pots, plant one stem for each inch of pot diamenter. Poke each stem an inch or two into the sand, and cover the planted pots with gravel to hold them down. Place them in wire cages, available from a water-garden supplier, if you have koi or other hungry fish. Place the pots so the plants are covered by 1 to 2 feet of water. At this depth, they will get enough light to survive. In deep ponds, place the pots on supports if necessary. Location is important, too. They don't like agitation, so you'll need to place them away from the pump.

When the plants are about a foot long, cut off half their length, and repot the tops in new pots. Once you have the recommended number of oxygenating plants for your pond's size, keep their growth in check with regular pruning.

Water Hyssop
(Bacopa caroliniana)
Zones 8–10. Native to southern coastal areas; light blue flowers appear above the water.

Fanwort Carolina Water Shield
(Cabomba caroliniana)
Zones 6–11. Fan-shape leaves are feathery underwater; linear and pointed above the water line.

Hornwort
(Ceratophyllum demersum)
Zones 6–9. Develops stems 1–2 feet long, covered in whorls of forked leaves.

Anacharis
(Egeria densa, also sold as Elodea densa or Anacharis densa)
Zones 6–11. Semievergreen; produces branched stems.

Hair Grass
(Eleocharis acicularis)
Zones 7–10 (but often hardier). Pale green, needle-like leaves create the look of an underwater lawn. Spikelike flowers.

Canadian Pondweed
(Elodea canadensis)
Zones 5–10. Hardy from Canada to the Deep South. Whorls of translucent leaves curl downward.

Milfoil
(Myriophyllum species)
Zone 9. Some milfoils aren't winter hardy. Farther north, substitute myriad leaf (*M. verticillatum*).

Understanding Plant Listings

The six plant categories listed in this chapter—Oxygenators, Floating Plants, Water Lilies, Lotuses, Marginal Plants, and Periphery Plants—include the common name followed by the botanical name and the USDA Hardiness Zones in which they thrive. See pages 108–109 for maps.

Floating plants create shade, making the water cooler for fish and giving them a place to hide and lay eggs. However, they do not do well in ponds with fountains or waterfalls because they need fairly still water.

Water lilies and lotuses are the most familiar floaters, but many others are equally beautiful. Floaters tend to prefer about six hours a day of full sun, although lotuses, water hawthorns, and pond lilies are tolerant of partial shade.

Many floaters, notably water lettuce, butterfly fern, mosquito fern, frogbit, common duckweed, and some Lugwiglia species, actually float freely in the water. Others, such as water lilies, lotuses, water hawthorns, water poppies, bogbeans, pond lilies, and floating hearts, are planted in pots.

Floaters should cover no more than 70 percent of the water surface, or in a large pond, only 50 percent. Otherwise, submerged plants won't be able to function properly. Skim off excess free-floating plants and prune plants in containers.

Containerized plants must grow in submerged pots of heavy garden soil or specialized mixes available from a water-garden supplier. Place them at the depth recommended by the nursery or supplier, and fertilize them once a month with an approved aquatic fertilizer.

Frogbit
(Hydrocharis morsus-ranae)
Zones 6–10. This free-floating species has shiny, 1-inch-diameter leaves and cup-shaped white flowers.

Floating Heart
(Nymphoides species)
Zones 6–11, depending on species. Thrives in relatively shallow water.

Water Lettuce, Shellflower
(Pistia stratiotes)
Zone 8. Shaped resembles romaine lettuce. Considered a noxious weed in southern states.

Water Hawthorn, Cape Pondweed
(Aponogeton distachyus)
Zones 6–9. Good for tropical gardens. Flowers are heavily scented.

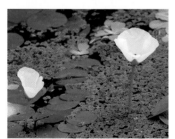

Water Poppy
(Hydrocleys nymphoides)
Zones 9–11. Has 3-inch pale yellow flowers and thick, glossy leaves.

Mosquito Fern
(Azolla caroliniana)
Zones 7–10. Also known as fairy moss. Green vegetation turns burgundy in autumn.

Pond Lily, Spatterdock
(Nuphar species)
Zones 4–11, depending on species. Globe-shaped flowers are followed by oval berries. *N. Pumila* is best choice for average-size water features.

Bogbean
(Menyanthes trifoliata)
Zones 5–11. Produces a foot-tall spike of fringed, star-shaped flowers in spring.

Water lilies are loved for their leaves, or pads, as much as for their blooms. The leaves are often purple or copper with splotches and streaks of other colors. Some have burgundy undersides, which show if the rim or a lobe edge turns up.

Water lilies are classified as either "hardy" or "tropical;" the tropical lilies are further divided into "day-blooming" and "night-blooming." Hardy water lilies are tolerant of Zone 4 conditions if the pond doesn't freeze at the level of their roots, while tropical water lilies are

hardy only in Zones 10 and 11. All water lilies have prominent central stamens and anthers, many in yellow and orange. Flowers are cup-shaped or star-shaped and single to fully double.

Choose water lilies based on leaf spread, flower color, and bloom time. Leaf spread is particularly important in small ponds where they can block sunlight. In tubs, you'll want a water lily with a spread of no more than 3 feet; in a small pond, a spread of 6 feet is good; a spread of 9 feet is appropriate for a medium-size

'Arc-en-Ciel'
Named for the rainbow; foliage ranges from deep pink to purple, yellow, green, and bronze.

'Escarboucle'
Flowers 6 inches, white-tipped red, spicy fragrance; leaves up to 11 inches; spread 4 to 5 feet.

'Charlene Strawn'
Large, star-shaped flowers, yellow, fragrant; leaves 9 inches; spread 3 to 5 feet.

'Froebelii'
Burgundy flowers 4 inches; leaves 6 inches; spread 3 feet. Good in shallow water.

'Chrysantha'
(formerly 'Graziella')
Flowers 3 to 4 inches, apricot to red-orange; leaves 6 inches, mottled; spread 2 to 3 feet.

'Gloriosa'
Cuplike flowers get redder with age, fragrant; leaves 8 inches; spread to 5 feet.

'Darwin'
(formerly 'Hollandia')
Flowers 7 inches, double, pink, lightly fragrant; leaves 11 inches; spread 4 to 5 feet.

'Helvola'
(sometimes listed as *N.* x *pygmaea helvola* or 'Yellow Pygmy')
Flowers 2 to 3 inches, semidouble, clear yellow; leaves 5 inches long; spread 2 feet.

pond; and for a large pond, 10 or more feet is about right.

Plant water lilies in a 12 to 18-inch-wide pot with good drainage or a specially made plastic basket in mid-spring unless you live in zone 10 or 11, where you can plant year-round. The soil should be heavy enough so it won't float away. Fill the container half-full; lay the rhizome on top; and add soil around it until just the growing tip is exposed. Some people add small gavel to the top of the pot, particularly if they have koi, but sharp lava rock cinders are a better choice because the lily has an easier time growing through them than through gravel.

Remove dead foliage and flowers before they rot and fowl the water. Fertilize with tablets available from aquatic suppliers. If pads grow above the soil surface, they are crowded and need to be divided. After unpotting the rhizome, wash it off so you can see the separate growing tips. Cut it into sections with growing tips and replant. Give extras away to friends; don't be tempted to fill your pond with more leaves than it can safely support.

'James Brydon'
Flowers 4 inches, double, rosy red, fragrant; leaves 7 inches, purplish to bronze; spread 3 to 4 feet.

'Rose Arey'
Flowers 7 to 8 inches, semidouble, deep pink, fragrant; leaves up to 9 inches; spread 4 to 5 feet.

N. x *marliacea* 'Carnea'
(also sold as 'Marliacea Carnea')
Flowers 5 inches, semidouble, pale pink; leaves to 8 inches; spread 4 to 5 feet.

N. *odorata* 'Sulphurea Grandiflora'
Flowers 9 inches, semidouble, bright yellow; leaves 11 inches, oval; spread 4 to 5 feet.

'Masaniello'
Flowers to 6 inches, bright pink; leaves 9 inches; spread 4 feet.

'Virginalis'
Flowers 5 inches, white; leaves 9 inches; spread 3 to 4 feet.

'Pearl of the Pool'
Flowers to 6 inches, double, pink, fragrant; leaves to 10 inches; spread 4 to 5 feet.

'Virginia'
Flowers to 8 inches, semidouble, white to palest yellow; leaves 10 inches; spread 5 to 6 feet.

Tropical water lilies are prized for their fragrance, as well as their good looks. Even if not hardy outside in most of the US and Canada, they can be wintered over and will bloom in climates with three or so months when the air temperature averages 65°F or above. To care for them during the winter, pull the pot from the water, and dump it on a clean surface. Gently remove the rhizome, and rinse it under lukewarm water. Let it dry for a few days, and then brush off the remaining soil. You can also remove excess roots. Store the rhizome in a container filled with distilled water in a cool, but not freezing, place for the winter. A couple of months before you expect the water in your pond to reach 70°F, pot up the rhizome, and place the pot in a pan of water on a windowsill. Keep it in bright light as it grows, and move it to the pond once the water temperature is 70°F. If this seems like too much work or you don't have the right climate, grow tropical water lilies as annuals each year.

'Afterglow'
Flowers 6 to 10 inches, yellow shading to orange, very fragrant; leaves 11 inches; spread 6 to 8 feet.

'Marian Strawn'
Flowers 9 inches, white, fragrant; leaves 15 inches; spread 7 to 8 feet.

'Aviator Pring'
Flowers 10 inches, semi-double, deep yellow; leaves to 12 inches; spread 6 to 8 feet.

'Pamela'
Flowers 8 to 13 inches, lilac-blue; leaves to 15 inches long; spread 6 to 8 feet.

'Blue Beauty'
Flowers 10 inches, semi-double, rich blue, fragrant; leaves to 15 inches; spread 4 to 8 feet.

'Panama Pacific'
Flowers 5 inches, red-violet; leaves to 11 inches; spread 3 to 6 feet.

'General Pershing'
Flowers up to 11 inches, double, lavender-pink, fragrant; leaves 10 inches; spread 5 to 6 feet.

'Yellow Dazzler'
Flowers 10 inches, double, bright yellow, fragrant; leaves to 17 inches; spread 6 to 8 feet.

Night-blooming water lilies tend to be large plants with leaves about 15 or 16 inches in diameter and an average plant spread of 10 feet in ideal conditions, so they are appropriate only for medium- and large-size ponds. Aside from their dramatic size, they are valued for their time of bloom. While most of the day-blooming water lilies close their petals before dusk, meaning that you can't enjoy them in the evening, night-bloomers open at dusk and close again at about noon the following day. So if you are away during the day but enjoy the garden in mornings and evenings, these might be your best choice.

'Emily Grant Hutchings'
Flowers 7 inches, semidouble, rose; leaves 12 inches; spread 6 to 7 feet.

'Mrs. George C. Hitchcock'
Flowers 10 to 12 inches, pink, fragrant; leaves up to 15 inches; spread 7 to 8 feet.

'H.C. Haarstick'
Flowers 12 inches, dark red, fragrant; leaves 16 inches; spread 6 to 12 feet.

'Red Flare'
Flowers 10 inches, deep red; leaves 12 inches; spread 5 to 6 feet.

'Missouri'
Flowers to 14 inches, white, fragrant; leaves 14 inches; spread from 6 to 10 feet.

'Wood's White Knight'
Flowers 12 inches, semidouble, white, fragrant; leaves up to 16 inches; spread 8 to 10 feet.

Other Tropical Lily Choices

- **'Bagdad'**
Flowers 8 inches, light blue petals with lavender sepals, dayblooming; leaves 10 to 12 inches; spread 6 to 7 feet.

- **'August Koch'**
Flowers 4½ to 5½ inches, blue petals with purple sepals, dayblooming; leaves 12 inches; spread 4 to 6 feet.

- **'Midnight'**
Flowers 6 to 8 inches, dark violet-blue, dayblooming; leaves 9 to 10 inches; spread from 4 to 6 feet.

- **'Antares'**
Flowers 6 to 10 inches, deep red petals and sepals, night-blooming; leaves 10 to 12 inches; spread 5 to 7 feet.

- **'Trudy Slocum'**
Flowers 6 to 8 inches, flat white, night-blooming; leaves 13 inches; spread 5 to 6 feet.

Lotuses are surprisingly easy to grow. They are hardy to Zone 4 in a pond that doesn't freeze at their root level and will bloom after about three months when daytime temperatures average 80°F, although they do not do well in climates where temperatures are routinely 90° to 100°F. Although there are only two species, *Nelumbo nucifera* and *N. lutea*, there are hundred of cultivars, most derived from *N. nucifera*.

The majority of lotuses are day-bloomers. On the day they open, they close again by mid-afternoon. But for the next two or three days, they remain open even at night. They are fragrant and are often huge. After the petals fall, the seedpod expands and turns brown. It's frequently cut for use in dried arrangements.

Plant lotus tubers in tubs about 18 to 36 inches wide and 9 to 12 inches deep. As with water lilies, drainage should be excellent so that the soil is adequately aearated. Tubers grow quickly, so plant them immediately after you purchase them. If you wait too long, they will grow a mass of runners and be difficult to handle.

Fill the tub with heavy soil to about 2 or 3 inches from the top. Lay the tuber on the soil horizontally, and add

American Lotus, Water Chinquapin
(*N. lutea*)
Flowers 7 to 11 inches, yellow; leaves 12 to 18 inches; height 2½ to 5 feet.

'Baby Doll'
Flowers 5 inches; leaves 9 to 11 inches; height 2½ feet.

Sacred Lotus, (Egyptian)
(*N. nucifera*)
Flowers 12 inches, usually rose, fragrant; leaves to 3 feet; height to 6 feet.

'Charles Thomas'
Flowers 6 to 8 inches, lavender-pink, fragrant; leaves 14 to 22 inches; height 2 to 3 feet.

Asiatic Lotus
(*'Alba grandiflora'*)
Flowers 12 inches, white; leaves 16 to 23 inches; height to 6 feet.

'Momo Botan'
Flowers 6 inches, rose-pink; leaves 12 to 15 inches; height 2 to 4 feet.

'Angel Wings'
Flowers 9 inches, white; leaves 18 to 24 inches; height under 4 feet.

'Mrs. Perry D. Slocum'
Flowers to 12 inches, pink with yellow or cream, fragrant; leaves to 23 inches; height 4 to 5 feet.

more soil, leaving about ½ inch of the plant's growing tip above the surface. Add ½ inch or so of sharp lava cinders to hold the soil down, keeping them away from the growing tip. Add four to six fertilizer pellets, and fertilize again every month until 30 days before frost. Place the tub so the growing tip is covered by 2 to 3 inches of water. If your pond freezes in winter, lift the lotus container out of the pond, and store it in a plastic bag in a location where temperatures remain about 55°F.

Marginal plants are the species that grow along the edges of ponds and streams. They like water over their roots for at least part of the year. Plant some on the edges of your water garden, either in containers at the edges or on plant shelves. They also grow well in tub gardens, particularly because all but the very largest and smallest do well in 2-gallon pots.

Plant them in heavy soil, covered with cinders of lava stone, and place them at the depth recommended by your supplier.

'Red Lotus'
(*N. nucifera var. rosea*)
Flowers 8 to 10 inches, rose-pink, fragrant; leaves 18 inches; height to 6 feet.

Sweet Flag
(*Acorus calamus*)
Zones 4–11. Strap-shaped foliage; leaves can grow 4 feet tall.

Double Rose Lotus
('*Rosea plena*')
Flowers to 13 inches, deep rose; leaves 18 inches; height to 5 feet.

Flowering Rush
(*Butomus umbellatus*)
Zones 5–11. Twisted, strongly vertical leaves; fragrant, cup-shaped, rose-pink flowers.

Tulip Lotus
('*Shirokunshi*')
Flowers 8 inches, white; leaves 18 inches; height 30 inches.

Bog Arum, Wild Calla
(*Calla palustris*)
Zones 3–8. Same family as jack-in-the-pulpit, with a flower similar to a calla lilly.

'Shiroman'
('*Alba Plena*')
Flowers 10 inches, cream; leaves 24 inches; height to 5 feet.

Marsh Marigold
(*Caltha palustris*)
Zones 3–7. Bright yellow flowers resemble buttercups; toothed, kidney-shaped leaves.

(continued on page 106)

(continued from page 105)

Marginal Plants

Green Taro
(Colocasia esculenta)
Zones 9–11. Elephant-leaved perennial; 2-foot, arrow-shaped leaves on 3-foot stalks.

Louisiana Iris Hybrids
(I. brevicaulis, I. fulva, I. nelsonii, I. giganticaerulea, and I. hexagona)
Zones 4–9. All five species have the same requirements. Colors include blues, purples, reds, yellows, and white.

Spike Rush
(Eleocharis montevidensis, also sold as E. palustris)
Zones 6–11. Also known as fiber-optic plant. Grows a foot high; produces a quill of small, brown tufts.

Cattail
(Typha species)
Zones 3–11
Dwarf cattail
(T. minima)
Zones 4–9. Flower spikes and long, pointed leaves are invaluable for water fowl.

Horsetail
(Equisetum species)
Zones 3–11. Grasslike plants with jointed hollow stems and brown cones at the tip. Grow in containers in up to 8 inches of water.

Yellow Flag
(Iris. pseudacorus)
Zones 4–9. Averages 3 feet tall; ribbed gray-green leaves; 3- to 4-inch yellow flowers in midsummer.

Cotton Grass
(Eriophorum species)
Zones 4–7. Resembles 2-inch cotton balls in mid-spring. Plant is 18 inches tall; height doubles with flowering spike.

Moneywort, Creeping Jennie
(Lysimachia nummularia)
Zones 4–8. Can grow in or out of the water; small, round leaves with bright yellow, cup-shaped flowers with dark red spots.

Chameleon Plant
(Houttuynia cordata)
Zones 5–11. Can be invasive, but useful in shade. Orange-scented, heart-shaped leaves.

Parrot's-Feather
(Myriophyllum aquaticum)
Zones 7–11. Related to milfoils; whorls of blue-green leaves above water surface, yellow-green below.

To create a pond that fits gracefully into your land-scape, add a surrounding zone of periphery plants just beyond the marginals. This scheme of pond and water plants, marginals, and then periphery plants, makes the pond and surrounding area seem more cohesive.

Periphery plants like high-moisture soils with excellent drainage. In nature, they grow far enough away from a body of water so that their roots are never covered with water. Both annuals and perennials fit into this category, but as you have no doubt discovered, you'll save time if you concentrate on perennials. Ferns and bulbs are good understory plants for the larger species and add interest to your design. Choose from the plants below, and keep scale and preferred growing conditions in mind. For example, you probably don't want a towering evergreen next to a small pond, or shade-lovers out in the open sun.

Umbrella Plant
(*Darmera peltata,* formerly *Peltiphyllum peltatum*) Zones 5–8. Round-topped clusters of pink or white flowers in spring that turn copper in autumn.

Ligularia
(*Ligularia species*) Zones 4–8. Grown primarily for their large leaves, but some species also bear showy yellow flowers.

Jack-in-the-Pulpit
(*Arisaema triphyllum*) Zones 4–9. Flower gives way to a stalk of scarlet berries. Plant in a cool, shady place.

Water Forget-Me-Not
(*Myosotis scorpioides*) Zones 4–9. Small, flat sky-blue flowers with an eye of yellow, white, or pink. Blooms in spring or early summer and reblooms throughout growing season.

Goatsbeard
(*Aruncus dioicus*) Zone 5. Grows 4 to 6 feet tall but is surprisingly delicate. Develops creamy white "beards" in late spring.

Spider Lily
(*Hymenocallis species*) Zones 6–11. White with six long petals; leaves grow about 18 inches tall; flowers are up to 5 inches across.

Astilbe, False Spirea
(*Astilbe species*) Zones 4–8. Fuzzy plumes are usually in the white-pink-red range, with a few salmons and lavenders. Range in height from 1 to 4 feet.

Chain Fern
(*Woodwardia species*) (*W. areolata*) Zones 4–8 (*W. virginica*) Zones 4–10 (*W. fimbriata,* also sold as *W. radicans*) Zones 8–10. A deciduous fern that creeps along ground rather than forming clumps.

zone maps

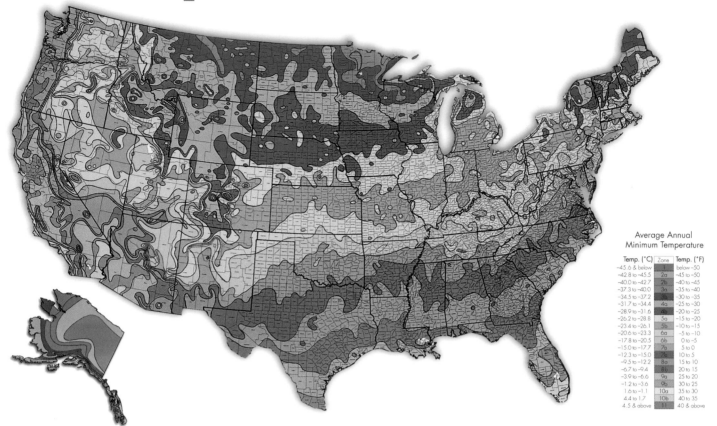

Average Annual Minimum Temperature		
Temp. (°C)	Zone	Temp. (°F)
-45.6 & below	1	below -50
-42.8 to -45.5	2a	-45 to -50
-40.0 to -42.7	2b	-40 to -45
-37.3 to -40.0	3a	-35 to -40
-34.5 to -37.2	3b	-30 to -35
-31.7 to -34.4	4a	-25 to -30
-28.9 to -31.6	4b	-20 to -25
-26.2 to -28.8	5a	-15 to -20
-23.4 to -26.1	5b	-10 to -15
-20.6 to -23.3	6a	-5 to -10
-17.8 to -20.5	6b	0 to -5
-15.0 to -17.7	7a	5 to 0
-12.3 to -15.0	7b	10 to 5
-9.5 to -12.2	8a	15 to 10
-6.7 to -9.4	8b	20 to 15
-3.9 to -6.6	9a	25 to 20
-1.2 to -3.6	9b	30 to 25
1.6 to -1.1	10a	35 to 30
4.4 to 1.7	10b	40 to 35
4.5 & above	11	40 & above

The USDA Hardiness Map divides North America into 11 zones according to average minimum winter temperatures. Hardiness zones are used to identify regions to which plants are suited based on their cold tolerance, which is what "hardiness" means. Many factors, such as elevation and moisture level, come into play when determining whether a plant is suitable for your region. Local climates may vary from what is shown on this map. Contact your local Cooperative Extension Service for recommendations for your area.

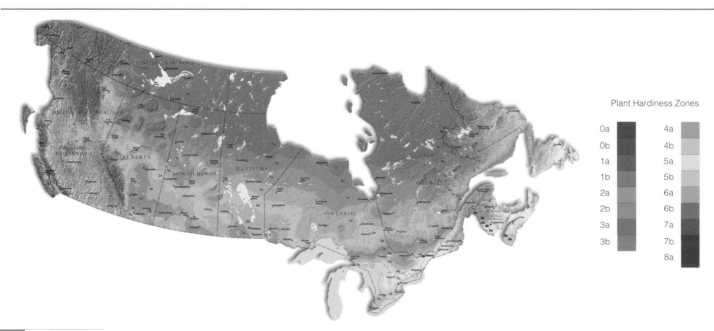

Plant Hardiness Zones

0a	4a
0b	4b
1a	5a
1b	5b
2a	6a
2b	6b
3a	7a
3b	7b
	8a

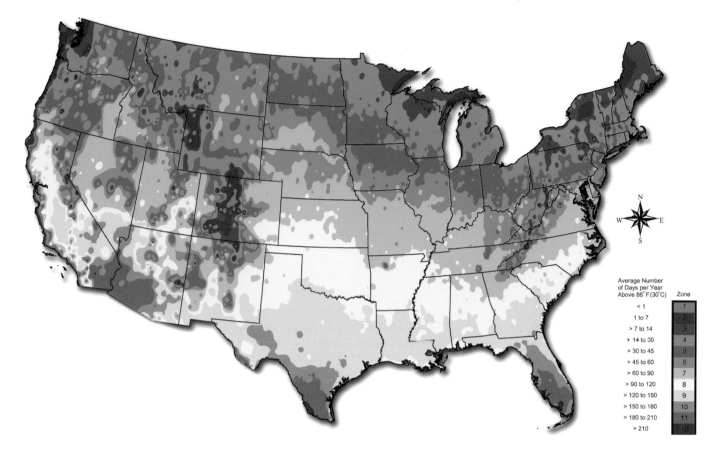

Average Number of Days per Year Above 86°F (30°C)	Zone
< 1	1
1 to 7	2
> 7 to 14	3
> 14 to 30	4
> 30 to 45	5
> 45 to 60	6
> 60 to 90	7
> 90 to 120	8
> 120 to 150	9
> 150 to 180	10
> 180 to 210	11
> 210	12

The American Horticultural Society Heat-Zone Map divides the United States into 12 zones based on the average annual number of days a region's temperatures climb above 86°F (30°C), the temperature at which the cellular proteins of plants begin to experience injury. Introduced in 1998, the AHS Heat-Zone Map holds significance, especially for gardeners in southern and transitional zones. Nurseries, growers, and other plant sources will gradually begin listing both cold hardiness and heat tolerance zones for plants, including grass plants. Using the USDA Plant Hardiness map, which can help determine a plant's cold tolerance, and the AHS Heat-Zone Map, gardeners will be able to safely choose plants that tolerate their region's lowest and highest temperatures.

Canada's Plant Hardiness Zone Map outlines the different zones in Canada where various types of trees, shrubs, and flowers will most likely survive. It is based on the average climatic conditions of each area. The hardiness map is divided into nine major zones: the harshest is 0 and the mildest is 8. Relatively few plants are suited to zone 0. Subzones (e.g., 4a or 4b, 5a or 5b) are also noted in the map legend. These subzones are most familiar to Canadian gardeners. Some significant local factors, such as micro-topography, amount of shelter, and subtle local variations in snow cover, are too small to be captured on the map. Year-to-year variations in weather and gardening techniques can also have a significant impact on plant survival in any particular location.

glossary

Acrylonitrile butadiene styrene (ABS) A plastic formulation (typically black in color) used for some rigid pond shells, also for drainpipe in plumbing systems.

Aeration The infusion of oxygen into water by mixing it with air, usually by means of a fountain spray or underwater air bubbler (such as those used in aquariums).

Algaecide A chemical treatment that prevents or controls algae growth.

Backfill Earth, sand, or gravel used to fill the excavated space around a pond shell or liner.

Balanced water Water with the correct ratio of mineral content and pH level that prevents an alkaline or acidic buildup.

Catch basin In a man-made stream or watercourse, a small depression or basin beneath a waterfall designed to hold water when the pump is turned off.

Chicken wire Flexible wire mesh used to reinforce thin concrete structures; also referred to as poultry netting. Sold in hardware stores, lumberyards, and home centers.

Chloramines Complex compounds formed when chlorine (from tap water) combines with nitrates present in pond water. Toxic to fish and plant life, chloramines are difficult to neutralize by chemical means—the pond water usually must be partially or fully replaced to reduce chloramine levels.

Conduit Metal or plastic pipe used to encase buried or exposed electrical cables and protect them from moisture or physical damage.

Coping Stones, bricks, or other individual masonry units used as a finished edging around the pond perimeter. Coping can be set loose or mortared in place.

Crown The growing tip of a root system, from which a plant sprouts; the point at which plant stems meet the roots.

Dry well A gravel-filled hole used to receive and drain water runoff; part of a drainage system to which water runoff is directed via a perforated drainpipe.

Ethylene propylene diene monomer (EPDM) A kind of synthetic rubber. Flexible sheets of EPDM are used for pond liners. EPDM has greater stretch and UV resistance than PVC.

Footing The widened, below-ground portion of a poured-concrete foundation or foundation wall.

Frost heave Shifting or upheaval of the ground due to alternate freezing and thawing of water in the soil.

Frost line The maximum depth to which soil freezes in winter; your local building department can provide information on the frost line depth in your area.

Game fish Large, usually carnivorous fish such as trout, bass, pike and catfish. Due to specific oxygen, space, and temperature requirements, game fish don't do well in small garden ponds.

Grade The ground level. "On grade" means at or on the natural grade level.

Ground-fault circuit interrupter (GFCI) A safety circuit breaker that compares the amount of current entering a receptacle with the amount leaving. If there is a discrepancy, the GFCI breaks the circuit in 1/40 of a second. The device is usually required by code in outdoor areas that are subject to dampness.

Head The vertical distance between a pump and water outlet, used to determine pump performance. Pumps are sized by how much water (in gallons per hour) they can deliver at different "head" heights above the water level of the pond.

Light well A lighting fixture recessed below ground level that directs light upward, typically used to highlight tall plantings or other features beside the pond.

Marginal plants Various plant species that grow in wet or boggy soil around the edges of a stream or pond.

Mil One one-thousandth of an inch; the measurement used to gauge the thickness of PVC and rubber pond liners.

Nitrifiers Beneficial bacteria present in pond water that break down fish wastes and other organic matter, transforming toxic ammonia into harmless nitrates, which nourish plants.

Oxygenating grasses Various species of submerged plants used primarily to add oxygen to pond water.

pH A measure of acidity or alkalinity of soil or water. The pH scale ranges from 0 (acid) to 14 (alkaline). Midpoint 7 represents neutral (neither acid nor alkaline). Healthy pond water ranges in pH from 6.5 to 8.5.

Photosynthesis The synthesis of carbohydrates by plants from carbon dioxide, water, and inorganic nutrients (nitrates and phosphates) using sunlight as an energy source.

Pier A concrete or masonry block rising above ground level to support the structure above it.

Plastic cement A dry cement mixture that includes a powdered latex additive to reduce cracking and serves as a waterproofing agent.

Polyvinyl chloride (PVC) A type of plastic formulation. Thin, flexible sheets of PVC plastic are used for pond liners. Rigid PVC plastic pipe is used for water supply lines.

Reinforcement bar Often called *rebar*. Steel rods used to reinforce thick concrete structures to prevent cracking.

Rhizome A spreading underground stem or runner, which forms the root stock for hardy water lilies and some other water plants.

Runoff Water traveling across the ground surface, caused by heavy rains or irrigation. If the surrounding ground is sloped toward a pond, surface runoff can wash dirt and garden chemicals into the pond.

Scavengers In garden ponds, creatures such as snails, mussels, clams, or tadpoles that feed on fish wastes, algae, and dead organic matter.

Sod Sections of turf or grass cut from a lawn (usually with a flat-blade shovel) that contain both the root system and top growth. Can be replanted if kept moist.

Swale A broad, shallow ditch or depression in the ground, either occurring naturally or excavated for the purpose of directing water runoff.

Topography The relief features or surface configuration of an area; the contour of the land.

Tuber The enlarged fleshy portion of an underground stem or rhizome; a potato is one example. Tropical lilies are tuberous plants.

Ultraviolet light (UV) Invisible rays at the extreme violet end of the sun's light spectrum, which cause color fading and deterioration of certain materials, such as plastics. Most pond liners have chemical additives to inhibit the effects of UV rays.

Underlayment A thick fabric material placed under a flexible pond liner to protect it from stones or other sharp objects in the pond excavation. Get underlayment materials from pond dealers.

Variance A formal waiver from a municipal building department or similar agency to allow an exception to local codes or ordinances on a nonconforming feature of a building project.

Weir A notched obstruction or spillway placed across a stream to create a waterfall.

index

Glossary/Index

Photo Credits

Illustrations by: Michele Angle Farrar

All photography by Jerry Pavia, unless noted otherwise.

Note Abbreviations:
DT = Dreamstime.com
GPL = The Garden Picture Library/Photolibrary
H. Armstrong Roberts = Robertsock.com
Bruce Coleman & Photos Horticultural = Photoshot
Tony Giammarino = Giammarino & Dworkin Photography & Styling

page 1: Mary L. Dolan **page 3:** *top* Songquan Deng/DT; *second down* Sergey Borisov/DT; *bottom* Tony Giammarino **page 5:** *top right* Vladimir Ivanov/DT; *bottom* Lisa Ewing/DT **page 7:** Lorna/DT **page 8:** *top* Robert Gubiani/DT **page 13:** *bottom* Mark Lohman **page 14:** Tony Giammarino **page 18:** *top right* Mark Lohman; *bottom* Tony Giammarino **page 20:** *all* courtesy of Beckett Corp. **page 21:** *all* Derek Fell **page 28:** *all* John Parsekian/CH **pages 31–33:** *all* Derek Fell **page 36:** *all* courtesy of Beckett Corp. **page 37:** *all* Derek Fell **page 38:** *bottom left* Tony Giammarino **page 44:** *all* courtesy of Danner Mfg. **page 45:** courtesy of Beckett Corp. **pages 49–52:** *all* Harry Heit/Steve Katona's North Hill Water Gardens **page 56:** *top center & top right* Tony Giammarino **page 57:** *bottom* Tony Giammarino **page 59:** Tony Giammarino **page 63:** *top* Mark Lohman; *bottom both* courtesy of Malibu Lights **page 64:** *right center* Mark Lohman **page 65:** *top* Jan Kranendonk/DT **page 68:** *top right* Ron Sutherland/GPL **page 71:** Jane Legate/GPL **page 72:** Alex Rakovsky/Dembinsky Photo Associates **page 74:** *top* courtesy of Beckett Corp.; *bottom* Gary G. Wittstock/Pond Supplies of America, Inc. **page 75:** Filip Fuxa/DT **page 76:** *top right* Tony Giammarino **page 77:** John Glover/GPL **page 78:** *top* Photos Horticultural; *bottom* Youssouf Cader/DT **page 79:** *all* Michael Howes/GPL **page 80:** Ken Druse **page 86:** *top left* Zhiwei Zhou/DT; *top right* Kodo34/DT; *bottom right* Göran Wassvik/DT; *bottom left* Popa Sorin/DT **page 87:** K. Rice/H. Armstrong Roberts **page 88:** Tony Giammarino **page 89:** Photos Horticultural **page 90:** *left* K. Rice/H. Armstrong Roberts **page 92:** *from top right* Chris Brignell/DT, *inset:* Göran Wassvik/DT; Ed Isaacs/DT; Kornilovdream/DT, *inset:* Zhiwei Zhou/DT; Popa Sorin/DT

Kodo34/DT **page 93:** *top left* James Craft/DT; *top right, middle right, bottom left all* Hans Reinhard/Bruce Coleman; *bottom right* E.R. Degginger/Bruce Coleman; *middle left* Michael Elliott/DT **page 94:** *top left* Venkatesan Parkunan/DT; *top right* Wuyi/DT; *bottom* Trudywilkerson/DT **page 96:** *bottom* Robert Pelham/Bruce Coleman **page 97:** *top left* Derek Fell; *top right* M. Timothy O'Keefe/Bruce Coleman; *bottom right* John Bova/Photo Researchers; *bottom left* Derek Fell **page 98:** *clockwise from top left* Bio-Photo Services; Filip Fuxa/DT; Derek Fell; Crystal Palace Perennials; Bio-Photo Services; E.R. Degginger/Photo Researchers; Bio-Photo Services **page 99:** *clockwise from top left* Hans Reinhard/Okapia/Photo Researchers; John Glover; John Glover; Nikita Tiunov/DT; Howard Rice/GPL; Dmitry Maslov/DT; Guodingping/DT; Denis Stenderchuck/DT **page 100:** *clockwise from top left* Svetlana Larina/DT; John Glover; Bluestock/DT; Jerry Pavia; Derek Fell; Sad444/DT; Vladimir Ivanov/DT **page 101:** *clockwise from top left* Ken Druse; Jerry Pavia; Perry D. Slocum; Jinfeng Zhang/DT; Kjell B. Sandved/Photo Researchers; Perry D. Slocum; Jessamine/DT; Lorna/DT **page 102:** *clockwise from top left* Mosaner/DT; Perry D. Slocum; Sasoykc/DT; Mike Brake/DT; Victoria Shaad/DT; Angiesart/DT; Infocus/DT; Videowokart/DT **page 103:** *clockwise from top left* Troutlake/DT; Konstantin Karchevskiy/DT; Ulrich Willmünder/DT; Dengyinchai/DT; Ina Van Hateren/DT; Peter Kirschner/DT **page 104:** *clockwise from top left* Rich & Galina Leighton/DT; Perry D. Slocum; Perry D. Slocum; Ctpaul/DT; Perry D. Slocum; Perry D. Slocum; Salma001/DT; Ti_to_tito/DT **page 105:** *clockwise from top left* Perry D. Slocum; David Cavagnaro; Howard Rice/GPL; Dmitry Maslov/DT; Arievdwolde/DT; Crystal Palace Perennials; Crystal Palace Perennials; Hurry/DT **page 106:** *clockwise from top left* Jerry Pavia; Sailorman/DT; Robin Keefe/DT; Dorien Windt/DT; David Cavagnaro; Jerry Pavia; Jerry Pavia; Inger Anne Hulbækdal/DT; David Cavagnaro; Michael Gadomski/Photo Researchers **page 107:** *top right down* Derek Fell; David Cavagnaro; David Cavagnaro; Stockshooter/DT; Jerry Pavia; *left all* David Cavagnaro